The Magic of Starting

The Science of Action, Momentum & Why Starting
Changes the Math

James Salas

Copyright © 2026 James Salas

Published by Headwaters Publishing
Printed in the United States of America

ISBN (paperback): 979-8-9929225-2-3

First edition.

This book is intended for informational and inspirational purposes only and does not constitute professional, financial, or legal advice.

For my wife and children,

who live with every start behind the scenes.

Acknowledgments

One influence stands above the rest. Edward de Bono's work shaped how I think and how I write. His clarity, directness, and refusal to soften ideas for comfort mattered to me. He challenged conventional thinking without worrying about stepping on toes—and did so with precision. I read his work closely and followed his ideas for years If this book feels unusually deliberate and direct at times, that influence is intentional.

Contents

Introduction

Most ideas don't fail.
They never begin.

A business concept stays parked. A career pivot waits for "better timing." A habit that would clearly improve your life never quite takes hold. A generous act gets postponed. A skill you know would compound over time stays untouched. Nothing explodes. Nothing collapses. It just doesn't start.

This book is about that gap.

Starting is often framed as something dramatic—a leap, a reinvention, a bold declaration. That framing does more harm than good. It inflates the cost of beginning and turns small, valuable actions into heavy commitments. In reality, starting is not a statement about who you are or where you're headed. It's a single, intentional action taken now.

When done correctly, it changes everything.

This applies far beyond "fixing your life." It applies to building habits that make you sharper, more reliable, and more useful. It applies to giving—your time, attention, effort, or resources—without overthinking it. It applies to developing character through repeated action, not intention. It applies to projects, businesses, creative work, and yes, to making substantial income over time.

Value compounds wherever starting is repeatable.

Most people don't stall because they lack ambition or discipline.

They stall because their starts are poorly designed. They wait for motivation to arrive, clarity to settle, or confidence to appear. But those things are not prerequisites. They are outputs. Motion creates information. Action produces confidence. Starting generates motivation.

This book is about reversing that sequence.

You'll learn how to make beginnings small without making them meaningless. How to lower the friction of starting so much that resistance has nothing to push against. How to restart quickly after interruptions instead of turning pauses into full stops. How to build systems where progress becomes the default, not the exception.

These ideas work at every scale. Starting a company and starting a daily habit follow the same rules. Building income and building character rely on the same mechanics. Giving consistently and creating consistently both depend on reliable entry points into action.

Nothing here requires hype.
Nothing requires force.
Nothing requires pretending the stakes are higher than they are.

This is about precision, not pressure.

Use this book when something would clearly add value—to your work, your skills, your income, or the people around you—but keeps getting delayed. Use it when you're thinking enough to feel busy but not enough to move forward. Use it when progress matters, even if the step itself is small. Everything big begins with a start you don't overthink.

PART I —Before the Start

Chapter 1 — The Smallest Start

Everything big begins small. Everything.

A towering oak started as a seed so light you could flick it from your fingertips. A thousand-mile river began as a trickle you could step over. Every story, every business, every family, every faith journey—each began with a first motion so quiet that no one clapped, no one noticed, no one cared. Except the one who started.

Most people never start because they think it needs to be big. Visible. Impressive. They imagine lights flashing, the perfect logo, the flawless plan. So they wait. And wait. And wait—until the dream itself quietly starves.

But the magic of starting isn't in grand entrances. It's in humble, ordinary beginnings. The small start is the only real start. It doesn't feel glorious. It often feels ridiculous. But that's the doorway. That's the signal. That's the proof you're not lying to yourself anymore.

A small start might be a prayer whispered in the dark, a first rep at the gym when you feel weak, a half-page of writing when your mind is blank, a phone call you've been avoiding, a first dollar dropped into a jar. It looks almost embarrassing from the outside. But inside, it's tectonic. It's continental drift. It's soul motion.

In the physics of life, the start carries a hidden power: it disrupts entropy. Without it, everything collapses into noise, distraction, and slow decay. With it, a new world begins. Starting is the only force strong enough to break through the default drift of disorder.

Philosophers have wrestled with this moment of beginning for centuries. Aristotle wrote that motion is the actualization of potential—the seed holds the oak, but only action releases it. Heraclitus claimed that everything flows, but the river only exists because something once stirred the ground and let the water move. Across ages, thinkers circled the same truth: a world at rest stays at rest until something, or someone, chooses to move.

Centuries later, Newton gave it mathematical teeth: a body at rest stays at rest until acted upon. Call it inertia. Call it resistance. Call it laziness. The label doesn't matter. The law stands. Nothing shifts until force is applied. Your smallest start is that force—the strike against stillness, the nudge that sets the avalanche, the match that makes a fire possible. You don't beat inertia with visions or affirmations. You beat it with one undeniable move.

Eastern wisdom pointed to the same law long before physics gave it language. Lao Tzu wrote that the journey of a thousand miles begins with a single step. It's quoted into cliché, but clichés survive for a reason: because they're true. Step one doesn't look like much, but the thousand miles don't exist without it. The entire road hangs on that moment.

You don't have to be amazing to start. You don't even have to believe in yourself very much. You just have to move once, even if the move is tiny. That's all it takes to puncture the stillness. There is no ceremony. There is no audience. There is only the moment—the moment when belief and action collide, even if they barely touch.

And here is the secret no one tells you: you won't feel ready. You won't feel clear. You won't feel worthy. Good. Start anyway.

The smallest start is not just a step forward. It is proof of life. A declaration against entropy. A refusal to drift. The claim that you are capable of new motion. The seed does not know the oak it will become, but it splits the soil anyway. The stream does not know the sea it will reach, but it flows anyway. You may not know your full path, but the smallest start contains it all.

This is why beginnings feel heavy. They carry the weight of everything that might come after. The first word on the page contains the novel. The first dollar saved contains the fortune. The first step onto the track contains the marathon. To outsiders it looks trivial. To insiders it's the hinge of destiny.

Starting is not about confidence. It's about truth—the truth that nothing grows without a beginning, that potential without action is decay, that even the faintest start holds the weight of a new world.

And that's why this book doesn't open with applause or ceremony. It begins with you, here, in this moment, faced with the same choice every creator, builder, leader, and believer has ever faced: drift or start.

You've already been waiting. You've already been drifting. And if you're honest, you know where that leads: more of the same, more entropy, more delay.

The smallest start may look ridiculous. It may feel beneath you.

But it is the only doorway—the only proof that you're willing to do more than dream. Every world that ever mattered began with a start so small it was invisible. Yours will too. Don't miss it.

I'm not promising you a miracle. I'm giving you a lens. Once you see the world through the power of beginnings, you stop hesitating and start acting. You stop drifting and start building. You stop waiting for the perfect moment and begin creating the moment. Everything shifts when you understand how starting really works, and if you stay with me through this book, that shift won't be theoretical. It will be lived.

Chapter 2 — The Moment Before the First Move

There's a unique electricity in the air just before something begins. Athletes feel it. Entrepreneurs feel it. Artists, leaders, teachers, parents—it doesn't matter the field. The moment before the first move is charged with tension. We think we need clarity. We think we need confidence. But what we really need is contact. We need motion to release the weight of anticipation.

Take football. Every player on the field, no matter how experienced, carries a bundle of nerves into the game. But they all crave the first hit. The first hit strips away the tension. It reminds the body and mind: the game is real now. You're in it. There's no more waiting. That collision, however painful, signals to the nervous system that it's time to focus and perform. The mental fog clears. That first hit is a physical gateway into presence.

Starting works the same way in life. Whether you're picking up a pen, starting a business, making a call, or walking into a new environment—what you need isn't more preparation. What you need is contact. That first move might not feel graceful or perfect, but it will shake you loose.

Neuroscience backs this up. In a 2018 study from the University of Freiburg, researchers found that action—any action—can reduce anxiety by disrupting worry-based rumination. When people were stuck in thought loops, initiating even a minor task helped reset the brain's threat detection system. Participants who physically moved, whether by cleaning or taking a simple step, experienced a measurable decrease in anticipatory anxiety. The researchers called this the "behavioral interruption effect"—meaning the brain has to disengage from fear-based projection when physical action begins.

This is why the moment before the first move feels heavy. It's a mental bottleneck. All your doubts compress into that single hesitation. But the moment you move—really move, not just plan to—you begin to break the cycle.

It's easy to mistake overthinking for preparation. But over-thinking is often disguised avoidance. We play mental chess, imagining every scenario, trying to predict outcomes, hoping we can game the system of life without ever stepping onto the field. But the field doesn't respond to thought. It responds to presence. And presence begins with movement.

Picture someone standing on a cold beach, shivering as they debate jumping into the ocean. They test the water with their toe. They circle the shoreline. They breathe deeply and tell themselves, "This is the day." But nothing changes until they run and dive in. That first full-body immersion shifts everything. In seconds, they go from watching the experience to living it. The first move transfers you from the mental world to the physical one.

This principle shows up in a study by Dr. Timothy Pychyl, a psychologist at Carleton University who specializes in procrastination. Pychyl's research demonstrated that people who simply started a task—especially one they had been avoiding—reported a significant drop in negative emotions immediately after beginning. Their mood improved. Their stress decreased. And most importantly, their perception of the task shifted. What once felt overwhelming became manageable—not because anything changed externally, but because action had been taken.

That's the magic: it's not the size of the step that matters. It's the signal that step sends. The signal is simple: I am no longer frozen.

In football, the first hit sets the tone. In life, the first move resets your brain. Both allow you to engage with the world instead of circling it in your mind.

When you're stuck, try this: name the smallest physical action you can take toward what's next. Not a strategy session. Not a whiteboard. A physical motion. Something you can do with your body that sends a message to your system: we're in this now.

It might be opening your laptop, putting your shoes on, dialing the number, or taking the dish out of the sink. Not as a metaphor—as a literal, real-world anchor. These small acts, insignificant as they seem, begin to collapse the mental fog. And in their place, they create motion. Because motion is clarity—not the other way around.

The modern world has conditioned us to seek certainty first. We want to have a vision board, a mapped-out plan, a mission statement. But those things often become delay tactics. The truth is, most of us don't need a better plan. We need a physical ignition.

Here's the shift: instead of waiting for inspiration to move,

move and let the inspiration catch up.

Before the first move, there's friction. It's real. You feel the weight of all your internal expectations—the doubts, the imagined criticism, the what-ifs. But motion is the release valve. It tells your nervous system: I'm safe, I'm present, I'm acting. And once the body is engaged, the mind aligns.

Don't wait for the nerves to disappear. Move through them. Don't try to think your way into confidence. Act your way into clarity. Confidence isn't a prerequisite. It's a byproduct.

The moment before the first move is your mind's last stand. It's resistance making one final plea. But it's also the birthplace of courage. Not because you feel brave—but because you act anyway.

Your task isn't to conquer the fear. Your task is to break the seal. Take the swing. Make the hit. And let the game begin.

This is why elite athletes train to move, not just to think. Practice is physical. Drills are not about hope. They're about muscle memory, timing, and readiness under pressure. In the same way, we train ourselves to start—not just once, but again and again—until starting becomes second nature. Until the first move is a reflex, not a debate.

Olympic diving isn't known for famous names — it's known for that one frozen second at the edge of the platform. Every broadcast circles this moment: the diver standing motionless, toes gripping the platform, the world quiet, the water still. They haven't moved yet. But everything depends on the next inch. This moment looks like meditation, but it's actually violence contained — the calm before the explosion of movement. People don't remember who dove. They remember that moment.

There's another reason this matters. Action reshapes identity faster than thought. When someone acts—even in a small way—they immediately begin to see themselves differently. This identity shift is subtle but powerful. It's the reason people begin to say, "I'm the kind of person who…" It doesn't come from journaling about your goals or listing your values. It comes from action repeated often enough that the brain updates the self-image to match the behavior.

A recent study from Stanford University found that people who adopted "identity-based habits" stuck with them far longer than those who simply had outcome goals. The researchers gave one group the goal of writing more. The other group was told to view themselves as "writers." The second group not only wrote more consistently—they reported higher satisfaction and stronger resilience. Why? Because the act of writing reinforced the identity of being a writer. Every time they wrote, they weren't just doing something. They were becoming someone.

The same applies to starting. When you start, you're not just moving forward. You're rewriting who you are.

So next time you feel that tension—when your chest is tight and your brain is clouded—don't wait. Don't try to fix your thoughts. Move. Make contact. That first hit, that first action, that first swing isn't about progress yet; it's about direction. Once that turn happens, everything that follows has somewhere to go.

Chapter 3 — Why Starting Is Harder Than Winning

Starting sounds easy. It isn't. It's harder than finishing, harder than winning, harder than almost anything else. Starting is the moment where raw reality hits resistance—not momentum, not applause. Just you and the first crack of effort. It's the step before rhythm, before recognition, before any of it feels worthwhile.

Ask anyone who's built something real—a business, a book, a relationship, a mission. The hardest part wasn't the sprint to the finish line. It was standing alone at the edge, putting something out into the world before anyone cared.

In 2002, Dr. Peter Gollwitzer at NYU ran a study on what happens in the brain when people announce versus act on their goals. Participants who publicly declared their intentions and received social praise were less likely to follow through. Their brains registered the praise as if they'd already succeeded. Meanwhile, those who kept quiet and simply started were far more likely to finish. The lesson was clear: saying isn't doing. Starting is.

This is where most people stall—in the fantasy. The name storming. The mental rehearsal. The branding package. They polish the mission statement no one asked for. Meanwhile, the ones who move forward send an invoice. They launch something imperfect. They sell. They learn. They adjust. They make contact with the real world while everyone else polishes imaginary greatness.

11

Bill Gates did this at the highest level. Before Microsoft was a household name, IBM needed an operating system. Gates didn't build one. He found QDOS, bought the rights, renamed it MS-DOS, and licensed it to IBM. No perfect product. No logo launch. Just guts, action, and momentum. That decision—to act before feeling ready—became the cornerstone of a company that reshaped the world.

Starting is harder than winning because there's no traction. No scoreboard or applause. Just motion through fog. Winning is rhythm. Starting is friction.

Look at New Year's resolutions. Every January, millions declare goals. Most abandon them within weeks. A 2021 Strava study confirmed that the majority quit by January 19th. The reason is simple: people confuse declaring a goal with building the muscle to act—starting again, starting when tired, starting without clarity. They want the identity without the initiation.

Every start feels like a tiny loss. You're slow. You feel out of place. You don't look the part. But the start is the soil where all progress takes root.

Writers know this. The blank page is brutal. It mocks you. But once you begin, the story grows. Athletes feel it in the first moments of a match. You're stiff, off-balance, unsure. But you move. And with movement, clarity comes.

A Harvard study compared visualization to practice. One group imagined themselves succeeding at a task—public speaking, performing, sports. Another group rehearsed. The visualizers felt more confident but performed worse. The practice group, despite lower confidence, performed better. The takeaway:

practice creates readiness. Visualization creates illusion.

A follow-up study from the University of Chicago showed the same pattern in numbers. Students who practiced free-throw shooting improved by more than 20%. The group who only visualized improved only slightly. Confidence alone didn't drive results. Motion did.

Starting forces you to break the false image of who you are. It reveals your gaps and demands you address them. That's why many people don't start—not because they can't, but because starting makes them see themselves clearly. They're not ready to know they're not as good as they imagined. Not ready to meet the reality of the marketplace. Not ready to fail in public.

But the irony is, those who start anyway end up becoming what others only imagine. They take the hit, feel the burn, and build something with muscle instead of mirage.

Take speaking. One man I knew spent years outlining topics, crafting decks, and polishing tag lines. But he never pitched an event. Never stepped onto a stage. His fear wasn't speaking—it was starting. Contrast that with a young woman who worked in a community college library. She began giving free lunchtime workshops on confidence-building and storytelling. The first time, only two people came. She forgot half her notes. But she showed up again the next week, and the week after. Word spread. The sessions grew. Eventually, she was invited to speak at a regional educators' conference—not because she waited to be called an expert, but because she started acting like one.

Sometimes the hardest part of starting isn't the action itself— it's what the action threatens. Your comfort. Your reputation.

Your self-image. It's easier to believe you could do something great than to risk finding out you're not quite there yet.

But here's the truth: greatness isn't discovered. It's earned. In the awkward starts. In the rough drafts. In the first rejections. In the silent rooms where no one claps. We often treat success like a light switch: off, then suddenly on. But starting reveals it's more like a dimmer—gradual, incremental, often frustrating. You don't leap into mastery. You grind into it. And every great success story has one thing in common: a beginning that didn't feel like success at all.

So if it feels hard right now—if you feel unsure or invisible or off the mark—good. You're not doing it wrong. You're doing it right. Because this part, the hard part, is the real beginning. The one that counts.

Chapter 4 — The Start You Almost Made

There's a strange ache that comes not from failure, but from never having tried. You carry it quietly—the memory of the thing you almost did. The business you nearly launched. The letter you drafted but never sent. The book with only a title. It's the echo of a start that never happened.

Everyone has one. Sometimes more than one. That career shift that felt too risky. That conversation that could have healed something. The volunteer work you talked yourself out of. And the longer time passes, the heavier the weight gets—not because of what happened, but because of what didn't.

Psychologists call this inaction regret. In a 2012 study by Gilovich and Medvec at Cornell, participants were asked to reflect on their biggest regrets. The results were striking: action regrets faded, but inaction regrets stayed. The vacation you didn't take. The business you never started. The love you never pursued. Those non-choices linger longest.

One man spent years planning to open a small Cuban café. He had a menu, a name, even sketches for the décor. But he never signed a lease. Life moved on. The café never opened. Years later he still spoke of it as if it were alive—but it existed only in his imagination.

Contrast that with a woman who wanted to run marathons but had never considered herself an athlete. One day, without much planning, she signed up for a local 5K. She didn't buy gear or follow a strict regimen. She just showed up. Finished near the back. But the race changed everything. She saw herself differently. Over time, she completed six full marathons. It all started with one small step she dared to take.

The start you almost made teaches you more than the starts you succeed at. It shows how close action is, how thin the line is between idea and execution, and how easily fear dresses itself up as logic.

People talk about fear of failure, but often it's fear of exposure—of being seen trying, of shedding the safety of the fantasy where you could do something great if you ever really tried. As long as the dream stays undone, it stays perfect. But action demands trade-offs: mistakes, feedback, vulnerability.

Still, action is the only path forward. A 2018 study in *Psychological Science* explored decision paralysis. Researchers found that people who took even small, imperfect steps toward a goal experienced more motivation than those who stayed stuck in analysis. Motion created momentum. Thinking alone did not.

The start you almost made doesn't just stay in memory. It shapes your future hesitation. You begin to identify with the version of yourself that doesn't follow through. That becomes the real threat—not failure, but a self-image of someone who never really tries.

You can trace entire chapters of life back to one moment you let pass. The job you didn't apply for. The meeting you canceled. The idea you sat on. The regret isn't just about the past. It's a signal about the present. If it still stings, it means you still care. Which means it isn't too late.

The pain of an almost-start can be a compass. It points to where energy still lives. The dream isn't dead. It's dormant. And regret is the reminder.

People often say, "If I had bought that house twenty years ago, I'd be a millionaire today." But the sharper question is this: What deal are you ignoring today that twenty years from now you'll wish you had started? The focus shouldn't be on the missed start behind you. It should be on the start you're neglecting right now.

It's easier to romanticize the past than to act in the present. Today's opportunity looks risky, unproven, uncertain. But so did that house twenty years ago.

Every leap begins small—a phone call, a meeting, an email, a first line written. Quiet, unseen, uncelebrated. But real.

The start you almost made will always whisper. But it doesn't have to define you. The only cure for an almost-start is a real one.

So do this: write down one start you've been avoiding. Then take the smallest physical step toward it today. Not tomorrow. Today. Because the only regret-proof decision is motion. And the only way to silence the ache of an almost-start is to begin

Chapter 5 — Starting Is Future Thinking, Not Present

Most advice about starting focuses on the present. Get in the moment. Be mindful. Just do it. But the truth is, most starts don't come from the present—they come from the future. Not from being grounded in now, but from believing in what could be.

Starting is a vote for the future. It's a wager. You act today not because the present guarantees it will work, but because you believe the future might. That belief, even if fragile, pulls you forward.

Think about why people start a business, write a book, or train for a marathon. It's not because today feels perfect. It's because they imagine a version of themselves months or years from now doing something meaningful. They project forward. They start not for now, but for later.

In 2014, Hal Hershfield at UCLA used MRI scans to study how people relate to their future selves. Participants saw images of themselves today and digitally aged versions. The brain lit up differently when viewing the older self—almost like it was a stranger. But those who felt more connected to that older version made stronger long-term choices, like saving and investing. The lesson: the more real your future self feels, the more likely you are to act in that person's interest.

Starting requires that connection. When the future feels real, you begin behaving accordingly.

This also explains why it's easier to act on impulse than on intention. The present self craves comfort and ease. The future self seeks growth and purpose. These two voices compete, and the loudest one usually wins. Starting happens when you quiet the present self just long enough to hear the other voice: *What if this works? What if this leads somewhere better?*

One man delayed launching his consulting business for over a decade. He had the credentials, the network, the skills. But he kept waiting for the perfect moment. What finally moved him wasn't advice or coaching. It was a mental picture—himself at 70, looking back with regret, not at failing, but at never trying. That image cut deeper than any fear of risk. The next day, he started.

Most starts aren't blocked by lack of knowledge. They're blocked by lack of connection to the future. You don't start because you haven't yet felt what's truly at stake.

A study in the *Journal of Experimental Social Psychology* showed this clearly. Participants were asked to visualize solving math problems. One group imagined only success. The other group imagined the steps—the struggle, the process. The process group outperformed the success group. Why? Because they built a mental bridge to the work. The others just fantasized.

That's the trap of blind positivity. It treats starting like a mood instead of a decision. But starting is practical. It's the first move in a sequence of real steps.

You don't need a hype man. You need a reason. Something ahead of you that matters more than the comfort of now.

That reason doesn't have to be grand. A young mother once decided to put aside five dollars a day. It wasn't much. But she told herself, *This is for my daughter's future, not mine.* Over time, the habit grew into real savings. That tiny daily start, fueled by her future vision, gave her the discipline she never found in the present.

Think about anything worthwhile you've ever done—school, work, relationships, children. You didn't begin those because the present was convenient. You began because you imagined what they could become. Vision pulls you through resistance, through fear, through boredom. It turns effort into investment.

But vision has to be specific. Not abstract. Not vague. Real enough to fight for. Sharp enough to guide.

So when you feel stuck, don't just ask, What do I feel like doing now? Ask, What does the future version of me need me to start today?

Then take one small step. Not because it feels good. But because it's good for the person you are becoming.

That's the truth about starting: it isn't about being present. It's about being faithful to the future. And the future always rewards those who show up early.

Chapter 6 — Don't Think Positive, Think Start

Positive thinking has its place. It can lift your mood, brighten your outlook, and shift your mindset. But here's the truth most self-help gurus won't say out loud: positive thinking won't move your feet. Starting—physically engaging with the world—is what separates the dreamers from the doers. Thinking has its role, but too often it's used to delay, to rationalize, to wait for the "right time" that never arrives.

You can visualize success all day. You can chant affirmations until your voice cracks. You can pin quotes to your wall and read them every morning. But if you don't take the first concrete action, you're just redecorating your mind while your life stays stuck in the same gear. Positive thinking gives the illusion of movement without the friction of actual change. It's a psychological warm bath—comforting, but it doesn't get you anywhere.

Starting is the only honest signal of change. And that's what people are truly craving—real, grounded change. The gym doesn't care how motivated you are. The manuscript won't write itself because you believe in yourself. The phone call that needs to be made won't dial just because you felt ready. Change requires a start, and starting requires nothing more than willingness. Not confidence. Not clarity. Just willingness.

There's a reason people feel better after taking action—even if it's a tiny, awkward move. Action breaks inertia. It snaps us out of autopilot and into motion. Once in motion, the emotions catch up. Once you're in the process, you become the kind of person who is doing the thing. The confidence you were waiting for shows up—but only because you acted.

In business, fitness, even relationships, people tend to wait. They wait for the spark. They wait to "feel ready." They wait for a mood shift or a sign from the universe. Meanwhile, someone else—someone with less talent or fewer resources—has already started. And because they started, they're building skill, they're building presence, they're becoming.

You don't need to believe everything will work out. You don't need to have all the answers. And you certainly don't need to feel 100% aligned before you act. That mindset is a trap. Starting with doubt, with nerves, with your knees shaking—this is the real entry point. Starting with uncertainty is not a flaw. It's the standard. People who win at the long game aren't those who had it all figured out from day one. They're the ones who moved anyway.

Take a student named Maria. She wanted to write her senior thesis but kept waiting to feel inspired. Weeks passed, and she had nothing. One night, instead of psyching herself up with another round of affirmations, she decided to write a single paragraph—just to break the block. That one paragraph turned into two. The next day, three more. By the end of the month she had a draft. Not because she thought positive, but because she started.

Even a false start has more value than a perfect plan sitting idle. Once you're in motion, you can adjust. You can pivot. You can gather feedback and redirect. If you stay in your head, you're locked in theory. Theory doesn't change lives. Starting does.

A 2011 study led by Gabriele Oettingen at NYU tested the effects of positive visualization on real-world outcomes. One group vividly imagined a positive future. Another focused on the obstacles in their way. The fantasy group performed worse. They felt satisfied just imagining success, so they didn't act.

In contrast, UCLA psychologist Shelley Taylor found that students who mentally simulated the process of studying—imagining themselves sitting down, opening the books, taking notes—outperformed those who only visualized getting a good grade. Process-based visualization primed action. Outcome-only visualization lulled people into complacency.

Because the brain often can't distinguish between imagined achievement and real action, positive fantasies can trick it into thinking you've already won, causing it to relax, while visualizing the process activates preparation and urgency. So if you're swirling in thoughts, trying to pump yourself up for the fiftieth time, stop—drop the script and take the smallest real-world action, not to finish it or win, but to prove you can move, because the point isn't the pep talk, it's starting the thing.

Chapter 7 — New Isn't the Start

There's a reason marketers slap the word *new* on everything. New flavor. New formula. New release. It triggers something deep in us—a pull, a whisper. Something in our wiring wants to believe that new means better, hopeful, clean, possible. But the truth most people never see is that *new* without action is a sedative. It keeps us shopping, scrolling, fantasizing. It gives us a cheap hit of dopamine, but it doesn't move us. Starting is what moves us.

Every new year, every Monday, every untouched notebook, every unopened gym membership—it's not the newness that matters. It's the start. There's something almost sacred about a fresh beginning. But most people misunderstand what makes it sacred. It's not the blank page. It's the first stroke of the pen. It's the movement. New doesn't transform. Starting does.

New is the cousin of start—similar energy, similar promise. They show up to the same party, but only one stays and does the work. We love to say, "I need a new job. A new routine. A new mindset." What we're really saying is, "I want to feel different without doing different."

But nothing changes unless we move. And sometimes the tiniest movement is enough to sanctify the moment. A single phone call. A single step into a gym. A single line written down. That's the key. New becomes real when you start.

Marketers know this. Apple doesn't say "better." They say "new." Car companies might talk reliability in the fine print, but their commercials still shout "new." Even cereal boxes do it.

Why? Because our brains crave novelty. Neuroscientists have shown that novelty spikes dopamine in the reward centers of the brain. But the buzz fades fast, and when the newness wears off, you're left with the same habits, the same body, the same mindset.

That's where most people quit. They think the magic was in the fresh start. But the magic is in persistent starting—over and over—not in novelty, but in motion.

Take the gym. One man bought expensive shoes, a smartwatch, even noise-canceling headphones—all still wrapped in their boxes. He kept waiting for the perfect day to begin. Another man showed up in worn sneakers and started with five push-ups. Guess who changed their body? Not the one with the new gear, but the one who started.

We chase new ideas, new services, new platforms. But all that newness can distract from the real work. Entrepreneurs sometimes tear down systems that are working just fine— because they got bored. They wanted new. Not better. Not deeper. Just different. But different doesn't always mean forward. Sometimes what you need isn't a new direction. It's to start again where you are.

That's the pattern of high performers and quiet re-inventors. They use newness as a trigger—not a destination. They start fast and stay consistent. They don't fall in love with beginnings. They fall in love with becoming.

And you can start over without changing your entire life. You can start again in the same relationship. You can start again in the same house, the same job, the same tools. You can even

25

start inside your own mess. You don't need a plane ticket. You need a decision.

The right kind of new doesn't ask you to abandon your responsibilities. It asks you to show up in them differently. New isn't the escape. Start is the entrance.

So if you want something new in your life, don't look outside. Look at what you can start inside.

Here's the punchline. Want a new body? Don't shop for gear—drop and give yourself twenty. Want a new mindset? Don't scroll quotes—sit in silence and face what's real. Want a new business? Don't pitch investors—start building the skill that solves a real problem. Every new life, every new outcome, every new joy begins the moment you start, because new doesn't transform—starting does.

Chapter 8 — The Mustard Seed Equation

We all love the idea of big wins—the tipping point, the viral moment, the sudden breakthrough. But anyone who has built something meaningful will tell you it didn't begin with a dramatic moment. It began with something so small it was almost invisible. That's the mustard seed principle: the smallest beginnings often hold the greatest potential, not because of their size, but because of their motion. In spiritual traditions, the mustard seed represents faith. In the mechanics of starting, it represents power. The force isn't in the seed itself; it's in what happens when it's planted.

People chase big surges of motivation, but momentum rarely comes from inspiration. It comes from a small, almost forgettable action taken at a moment when stopping would have been easier. I kept seeing this pattern over and over again. In my own work. In clients. In friends. In people who changed their careers, their bodies, their finances, their futures. The ones who won weren't the ones who made the biggest moves; they were the ones who made the smallest moves reliably.

At some point, after watching these patterns repeat themselves in different lives and different fields, I realized the entire psychology of starting could be reduced to a simple equation— one that captured the mustard seed principle with more clarity than any motivational slogan ever could. I began calling it **The Mustard Seed Equation**.

$M = A \times B \times C$
Momentum = Action × Belief × Consistency

Equations get remembered. They travel. People repeat them

27

because they're clean. We quote $E = mc^2$ because it's tight and undeniable. Engineers remember conservation laws because they're structured. So I gave this idea the same treatment—not to be clever, but because this concept deserves the clarity and permanence that only an equation brings.

Each variable is a multiplier. Action is the smallest physical move forward. Belief is the thread of possibility—not confidence, just enough signal to act. Consistency is the decision to return tomorrow. If any variable drops to zero, the whole system collapses. When all three are present, even in microscopic doses, they compound. That compounding effect isn't poetic. It's scientific. Systems theorists and behavioral researchers agree that small, repeated inputs outperform dramatic one-time efforts because they lower friction. Compounding interest works the same way. Chemistry works the same way. Ecological growth works the same way. Big outcomes emerge from tiny forces repeated over time. Starting behaves like a growth system, not a motivational slogan.

A young man I knew wanted to improve his health. Instead of redesigning his lifestyle, he committed to one push-up a day. Just one. The action created belief. Belief supported consistency. Consistency multiplied the action. Within months, he was unrecognizable. His transformation wasn't luck; it was A × B × C accumulating. But this principle doesn't only live in personal change. It thrives in business too. A realtor I worked with decided to make one meaningful outreach call every day. Not five. Not twenty. One. In a year, that single action produced three listings, a referral chain, and a completely different income level. He didn't reinvent his brand or overhaul his marketing. He planted a seed daily, and the return matured.

People underestimate these tiny beginnings because they're

quiet. They don't feel powerful. They don't feel official. But tiny is sustainable. Tiny bypasses perfectionism. Tiny builds identity through action, not daydreams. The seed never looks like the tree, but every tree begins in the same humiliating place: covered in dirt, unseen, ignored. Writers freeze because they expect the first session to feel meaningful. It rarely does. One true sentence outweighs a month of outlining. Fitness works the same way. Finances too. Health. Faith. Leadership. Creativity. Everywhere you look, lives change because someone took a small step and repeated it long enough for the compounding to kick in.

Every breakthrough—every business, every transformation, every reinvention—began as a seed planted by someone who decided the small start was enough. The Mustard Seed Equation gives structure to that truth. You don't need dramatic beginnings. You need daily beginnings. The question is no longer whether small starts work. It's whether you're willing to trust one long enough to let it grow.

PART II — The Weight of Inertia

Chapter 9 — The Power of the First Hit

There's a psychological shift that happens the moment your effort meets real-world friction. Before that point, everything exists in your head—plans, simulations, imagined conversations. You may feel nervous, but it's all internal. Nothing outside of you has pushed back yet. And that's the problem. Because no matter how much you rehearse, you're not truly in the work until something collides with you.

The first hit isn't a punch or a tackle. It's the awkward silence after your first cold call. It's the flat "not interested" after a pitch. It's posting something online and watching it sit there without a single response. It's the tiny shock that tells you: this is no longer theoretical. You're in the ring now.

People talk endlessly about confidence and mindset, but they ignore this essential pivot—the moment of impact. The real beginning isn't the decision to start. It's the contact between your intention and the world's response. Most people avoid that moment. They polish, delay, adjust, and rationalize. They say they're not ready. What they're really avoiding is the hit.

Psychologists understand this better than most. Exposure therapy doesn't cure fear by positive thinking. It works by contact: first a picture, then a room, then the real thing. Step by step, the brain re-calibrates through impact, not imagination. The first hit does the same thing. It shows you the truth: you can survive contact.

Leon Festinger's theory of cognitive dissonance explains why. When your action contradicts your fear narrative, the brain can't hold both beliefs. It has to update something. After the first call, pitch, or published post, the internal story shifts: I guess that wasn't as bad as I thought. The first hit punctures the illusion that fear is an accurate forecast.

That's why the second time feels easier. The third becomes familiar. The tenth becomes momentum. The world didn't change—your interpretation did.

The first hit shows up everywhere. The silence after sending a draft. The adrenaline crash after stepping on stage. The discomfort of your first listing presentation with a stranger. The cringe of hearing your recorded voice. It always feels awkward, but it also breaks the loop that keeps people stuck. Once the hit lands, the mind adjusts and the body steadies. Movement becomes natural again.

One creator avoided video for over a year. He had the skill and the message, but not the nerve. When he finally posted, the reel got six views—two were his own, one was his mom, and the rest were accidental. It didn't matter. The hit landed. A month later he was posting every other day. Not because the audience grew, but because the fear shrank.

That's the real power of early contact. It kills perfectionism. It collapses overthinking. It forces you into reality. Even rejection becomes data. Even silence becomes calibration. But most importantly, you prove you can take the impact.

Avoiding the hit only inflates it in your mind. You imagine humiliation, disaster, or some magical breakthrough—none of which are accurate. The actual hit is smaller and more useful. It strips away fantasy and places you in the only world where progress can happen.

Here's the principle: whatever you're resisting most is probably the hit you need—the phone call, the video, the conversation, the pitch. You can't theorize your way past the moment of impact; you have to meet it. The first hit won't kill you, but it will wake you up, and since the hit is coming either way, take it on your own terms and start there.

Chapter 10 — You Can't Think Your Way into Motion

Planning feels productive. It creates the illusion of progress. You outline the steps, you sketch ideas, you imagine outcomes, and for a moment it feels like you're already moving. But planning is not movement. It's a warm-up. A simulation. A rehearsal for a performance that hasn't started yet. And the danger is simple: the simulation feels so good—so structured, so safe, so controlled—that people confuse it with actual momentum. They're not in motion. They're in theory.

Real motion begins with action. Not with thought. Not with clarity. Not with confidence. With action. The hard truth is that most people try to think their way into courage. They engineer plans to avoid discomfort. They research to delay responsibility. They wait for a day when they'll "feel ready," but readiness doesn't lead. It follows. Action comes first, and everything else trails behind it.

Psychologist Timothy Pychyl, who has spent his career studying procrastination, put it in plain terms: motivation follows action, not the other way around. Once you begin—even a tiny beginning—the resistance starts to lose its teeth. The energy you were waiting for appears. The dread quiets down. The work becomes approachable, not because the task changed, but because movement rewired your internal state.

This is why thinking often becomes the enemy of doing. You can sit for hours thinking about writing a page and still end the day with nothing. You can talk for months about a business idea and never send a proposal or buy a domain. The mind is a master lawyer—it will argue endlessly that your stalling is actually preparation. It will let you research, plan, doodle, and debate every angle of a goal without ever forcing you to engage with it.

You want clarity? Move.
You want courage? Move.
You want discipline? Move.

Almost every trait people chase—confidence, certainty, flow, focus—is a lagging indicator of motion. Action manufactures the internal qualities people assume they need beforehand.

The mind tries to sell the opposite story. It warns that starting is reckless. It insists that you need more data, more certainty, more rehearsals. But clarity lives on the far side of action. You don't wait until you believe you can do something. You act, and the belief forms as a result.

This is where meditation becomes useful—not because it adds more thought, but because it interrupts thought. Meditation shuts down the mental spin cycle. It creates a boundary where the loops break and the brain stops negotiating with itself. Meditation is not about solving the problem in your head; it's about clearing the static so you can move without the mental fog.

I knew a young graphic designer who talked for months about launching a freelance business. She researched software, studied portfolios, drafted brand colors, sketched possible logos. But everything lived in her computer. She was planning her way into paralysis. One afternoon, she sent a single cold email offering to design a flyer for a local business. That small action—not the six months of planning—was the pivot. Within a week she had a client. Within a month she had two. Her life didn't change because she figured it out. It changed because she acted.

This is how systems actually get built. James Clear once said, "You don't rise to the level of your goals. You fall to the level of your systems." And systems aren't created by perfect plans. They're created by repetition—by doing the same meaningful action enough times that it becomes structural. The first repetition only happens when you start.

If you're stuck, the remedy is almost never more thought. It's less thought. You don't need better priorities. You don't need a new planning method. You need movement. One email. One call. One paragraph. One rep. That's how people unstick their lives—by stepping, not by thinking.

Thinking is the steering wheel. Action is the engine. And a steering wheel without an engine is just a prop.

The trap is that thinking feels responsible, even adult—you're planning, preparing, weighing consequences—but it can quietly become a cul-de-sac, a closed loop of potential energy with no ignition. The brain will let you stay there indefinitely because thinking protects you from the hit, the friction, the exposure of doing something real, and that's why you can't think your way into motion; you have to move your way into clarity and start there.

Chapter 11 — The 3-Second Rule

The start doesn't wait for you to feel ready. It waits for you to move. That's the real divide—not between success and failure, but between engagement and drift. Between momentum and entropy. Between becoming someone who shapes their life and someone who watches it happen from the sidelines.

People think starting is about motivation or clarity or confidence. It isn't. Starting is about micro-initiation—tiny, physical actions taken inside a narrow window. You think it, you move. Not in five seconds. Not after you've poured the coffee. Not after you've negotiated with yourself. Right now. Within three seconds.

Three seconds is the window. Any longer and the mind steps in with its usual sabotage. The brain is built to preserve energy and avoid risk. Give it four seconds and it will generate ten reasons to delay. It will inflate the task, invent fears, and reframe a simple action as something that needs more time, more preparation, more certainty. But if you act before that machinery spins up, you slip through clean. You bypass the hesitation loop entirely.

That's the point of the three-second rule. It isn't about rushing. It's about getting ahead of the psychological drag—the micro-paralysis that happens when you let hesitation harden. When you move inside the window, you override the identity that wants to stay still and reinforce the identity that takes action. The shift is subtle, but over time it becomes structural. You become someone who moves.

A woman once told me she wanted to start a podcast. She bought gear, researched hosting platforms, outlined episodes—everything except hitting record. She was waiting for confidence that was never going to arrive first. One afternoon she tried something different. She counted down: 3...2...1... and hit record on her phone. No script, no microphone, no plan. She rambled for five minutes and hated half of it. But she uploaded it anyway. That single, shaky episode led to dozens more. Within a year, thousands of downloads. Nothing magical happened except micro-initiation. She beat hesitation by acting inside the window.

This is what the three-second rule gives you: a bridge across resistance. Not a system, not a philosophy—just a flick of movement that cracks the inertia. Stand up. Open the file. Walk outside. Say the first line. That's all it takes to tip the scales from thinking to doing.

Psychologists talk about "action bias," the tendency to feel better after taking a step, even a small one. Neuroscientists tie it to fear circuits in the amygdala and the way action disrupts anxiety loops. Strip away the language and you're left with one truth: movement rewires emotion. You cannot think your way into action, but you can act your way into clarity, confidence, and momentum.

That's the second benefit of micro-initiation. Every time you move inside the window, you're reinforcing a new self-image. You stop being the person who hesitates and become the person who initiates. Repeat that often enough and it becomes your default setting. Not driven by motivation. Not driven by hype. Driven by identity.

Three seconds. That's all you need to change the trajectory of a moment. And moments compound.

So the next time you feel stuck, don't negotiate with the hesitation or analyze or wait for alignment or inspiration—just count down: 3...2...1...go, and move your body before your mind catches up. You're not trying to win the day; you're trying to start it, because once you start, the rest tends to follow, and the three-second rule isn't about starting fast so much as becoming someone who no longer waits.

Chapter 12 — Start Alone

Most people don't start because they're waiting for company. They think momentum needs permission, that movement needs applause. But if you're waiting for someone to join you, you're not starting—you're stalling. The things that actually moved the needle in my life all began the same way: silence, uncertainty, and no witnesses. Just me and the next step.

I remember the first time I filmed a real estate video by myself. The lighting was off, the audio was rough, and I wasn't sure it would even upload. But I picked up my phone, walked into the street, pressed record, and spoke like it mattered. That 90-second clip didn't go viral. But it produced my first social media lead. She said, "You reminded me of a friend. Just speaking the truth. So I reached out." That moment stayed with me. It taught me that starting alone builds credibility not because others believe in you, but because you prove you believe in yourself.

Psychologists call this the self-validation effect—the idea that decisive behavior creates confidence rather than requiring it first. A 2010 study at Ohio State found that people who acted boldly without external validation internalized more confidence afterward. The confidence didn't lead the action. The action created the confidence.

In a world obsessed with collaboration, masterminds, networking, and constant feedback loops, the solo starter is underestimated—and often more dangerous. You don't need a partner to validate your direction. You don't need a team to approve your path. Those things can come later. The real magic belongs to the person who moves before they're seen.

40

That's the hidden advantage of starting alone: no one's watching yet. You're free to be terrible, free to experiment, free to iterate without pressure. You can build in public or in private, but either way you're building without the weight of expectation. And technology makes the solo path even more powerful. One person today can write the book, build the site, run the ads, shoot the video, track the analytics, and collect the payments. You don't need capital or coworkers. You need a start.

Here's a prediction: the world's first one-person billion-dollar company will appear in the next decade. It won't come from Silicon Valley boardrooms. It'll come from a spare room or a garage. Ugly at first, ignored at first, but started nonetheless. And it will prove what has always been true: permission was never required.

History glamorizes the solo achiever after the fact—the visionary, the maverick, the misunderstood genius. But in real time, those people weren't admired. They were doubted. They looked like outcasts. They didn't fit. That's the price of building something before others can see it. You won't be celebrated. You won't be recognized. You may even be dismissed. But invisibility is a gift. It lets you make mistakes cheaply and learn quickly. It gives you space to develop muscle before anyone is paying attention.

The paradox is that when you start alone, you rarely stay alone. The momentum attracts the support. It never works the other way around. One of the great killers of movement is the idea that you need consensus first. You poll the group, wait for buy-in, dilute the spark, and by the time everyone agrees, the energy is gone. Solo starters bypass that entire trap. They don't ask, "What do you think?" They ask, "What's the next move?"

That's the mindset you need. Shrink the world. Close the circle. Cut the noise. You don't need feedback right now. You don't need applause. You need action. Start writing the book. Start filming the video. Start building the landing page. Start calling the leads. Start walking the farm. Start praying again. Start the habit no one else sees.

Some of the wisest people in history began in isolation— monks, philosophers, seekers of every tradition. They weren't hiding. They were building an inner structure strong enough to carry an outer mission. The same dynamic still applies. Starting alone forces clarity, discipline, and direction in a way group energy can't touch.

The coaching explosion of the last fifteen years only reinforces this idea. There's a coach for everything—health, dating, productivity, business. But most people don't hire a coach because they lack information. They hire one because they don't trust themselves to begin solo. And yet with all the advice in the world, millions still stay stuck. Why? Because information isn't transformation. Starting is.

If you're always waiting for a team, you'll be waiting forever, because the team doesn't create the momentum—the momentum creates the team. Start alone; it's the purest form of strength and the way almost everything real begins.

Chapter 13 — Start Before You're Ready

You're never going to feel ready—not for the big stuff, not when it matters. The more important the move, the more likely you are to feel underprepared. That feeling isn't a flaw in the plan; it *is* the plan. The myth is that readiness comes first, that if you read enough, research enough, or rehearse enough, you'll eventually reach a green-light moment. A cosmic signal. A point of certification.

That moment never arrives.

The people who start, the people who win, the people who change things—all begin in the same state: not ready. They move anyway.

I remember listing my first $4 million waterfront home. Until then I'd handled mid-range listings. Suddenly I was walking into an architect-designed estate with marble floors and sweeping bay views. I rehearsed the conversation a hundred times. I still had butterflies. But I showed up, over-prepared the marketing, walked the property like it was mine, and closed the deal. That sale didn't just elevate my business. It changed how I saw myself. It became the bridge to bigger opportunities. Today I'm working on a $30 million listing. I still feel a flicker of doubt—but now I know readiness doesn't come first. It follows movement.

I've watched this play out in my body as well. When I battled frozen shoulder, I could barely lift my arm. I started hanging from a pull-up bar. At first I couldn't hold my weight. My goal was ten clean pull-ups. Today I can do one—but ten will come, because I started. Then I made a promise to a younger friend of mine—stronger than me on the track. I told him I'd race him. One mile. My goal is to break six minutes. At 67, that number isn't casual; I used to run sub-six routinely in my high school and college days. I'm not there yet, but the challenge lit a fire. It gave me a reason to lace up and move.

There's a name for the mental block that keeps people from beginning: the illusion of competence. Research from Columbia and Yale shows that high achievers often wait until they feel 90–100% ready before taking action. Meanwhile, the most successful entrepreneurs and operators typically launch at 40–60%. They trust they'll build the wings on the way down. The military has its own version: operate at 70% certainty. If you wait to know everything, the moment is gone.

This is why so many talented people stay stuck. They loop in preparation—more books, more courses, more frameworks, more coaching calls. But starting isn't a knowledge problem. It's a courage problem. And courage only appears *after* the start. Even the imposter syndrome can become fuel. Studies show that founders who feel like imposters often perform better early on because once they commit, they over-prepare. But that edge only activates when you move.

Another damaging myth is that clarity must come before action. It feels responsible, but it's wrong. Clarity is a result of action, not a prerequisite. This applies to creative, professional, and personal work—if something involves real physical risk, you train first. But in the arenas that shape your life, clarity still follows movement. You figure out what you believe by doing. That's how my writing began. I didn't have an audience in mind. I didn't have a content strategy. I posted a line. Then another. People responded. The clarity came afterward.

Readiness is a lagging indicator. The more you act, the more ready you feel. Not the other way around.

School teaches the opposite. Study first, act second, evaluate third. But life flips the sequence. Action creates feedback. Feedback creates learning. Learning creates confidence. So if you feel unready, that's not a sign you should wait. It's a sign you're in the exact position where starting matters most.

Here's what no one says: starting too early is almost never fatal. But starting too late usually is. The window closes, the idea goes stale, someone else launches it, your energy drops, the doubt multiplies. Opportunity decays. And once it decays, it rarely regenerates.

Starting before you're ready generates energy. People notice someone in motion. Resources shift toward you. The start itself pulls opportunity out of the shadows. That's the real danger of waiting—it kills your edge.

When I launched *The Call of the Creek*, I wasn't ready. I wasn't sure about the cover. I didn't have a PR plan. I didn't know how readers would respond. But I published anyway. And the result was momentum—organic sales, reviews, reader messages. It wasn't perfect. But it was real. And real beats perfect every time.

Stop looking for the perfect moment. It doesn't exist. And even if it did, you'd miss it while preparing.

The ones who move ahead aren't braver, more knowledgeable, or more aligned; they simply move while scared, starting in uncertainty instead of planning in circles. Do it before you're ready—that's the start that counts.

Chapter 14 — Learning Can Be a Trap

I once spent six weeks studying how to build a podcast studio. I researched mics, arm stands, preamps, and acoustic foam. I compared platforms—Libsyn, Buzzsprout, Riverside. I joined forums. I watched hours of YouTube breakdowns. I even bought a course called *Your First Podcast: Launch with Confidence*.

Want to guess how many episodes I recorded?
Zero.

But I knew a lot. I could walk you through mic placement, vocal chains, and publishing workflows. I just never hit record.

That's the danger of learning. We've been trained to believe learning is always noble and always productive. Often it is. But for many people—especially smart, curious people—it becomes something else: a respectable form of procrastination. It feels like progress. It protects you from risk. You don't have to ship anything, commit to anything, or find out if your work is any good. You can stay parked in preparation, and no one questions it because you're "still learning."

But if you've been saying that for six months, you're not learning anymore. You're stuck. And stuck is death for starters.

Carol Dweck's work on the growth mindset showed that students who believed ability could be developed through effort outperformed those who saw intelligence as fixed. Important insight—but many people twisted it into a lifelong permission slip to stay in the shallow end. They turned "I'm learning" into a badge of honor and then never left the classroom. Learning became the goal instead of growth.

A Columbia Business School study by Erica Bailey and Daniel Bartels exposed the trap even more clearly. Researchers found that people often delay action under the guise of "gathering more information." But they weren't delaying because it helped them make better decisions. They were delaying because starting made them feel exposed. The term was elegant and brutal: information avoidance disguised as preparation. And the longer people delayed, the less likely they were to ever return. Their brain had already earned its dopamine hit from fantasizing about the project, so it lost the urgency to actually do it.

The smarter you are, the more vulnerable you are to this trap. The knowledge loop feels good. It stimulates. It keeps you safe. Readers, seekers, autodidacts—the bookstore crowd—they're the most at risk. They don't buy one book. They buy five. On five topics. Then convince themselves they're "going deep," when the truth is the opposite: the deeper they go, the more paralyzed they become.

Learning is pleasurable because it reduces uncertainty. It gives you the illusion of control. But starting forces you straight into uncertainty with no map. It makes sense that people cling to knowledge—they're wired to avoid the fog. Learning looks like it solves the fog. Starting magnifies it.

I've met people who can quote Seneca, Kahneman, and Naval—but still haven't launched a website. People who've read four books on productivity and still haven't made the call. Because when you stack knowledge on top of knowledge without doing, all you're really building is a mental weight that crushes momentum. You become smarter and slower at the same time.

What you need isn't more input. You need activation. Learning should follow doing—not block the entrance to it.

After my podcast failure, I made myself a deal. No more research. I hit record. The first episodes were rough. I stammered. The audio was uneven. The editing was garbage. But I published them anyway. And within a few weeks I had something six weeks of research couldn't give me: a real podcast. More importantly, I had momentum—confidence born not from learning but from action. That's when I realized most of my breakthroughs didn't come from study. They came from starting.

I wrote a phrase on a sticky note after that: "I only learn what I earn."
That became my rule. If I hadn't taken a step, I didn't deserve the next layer of information. I had to earn the right to learn.

It changed everything. I started filtering my curiosity through execution. If I couldn't apply it in real time, I ignored it. If I wasn't shipping, I wasn't studying. No more hoarding knowledge like future currency. Action was the currency.

Here's the truth: you will never feel ready. There will never be a moment where your knowledge feels complete, your tools are perfect, and your confidence is sky-high. Readiness doesn't come first. Completion does. And completion requires beginning.

Readiness is a myth sold to people who are terrified of failing.

But you *will* fail. That's part of the trade. The faster you accept that, the faster you move. The trap is believing you can avoid failure by learning more. You can't. You cannot learn your way out of uncertainty. You have to walk through it.

Every successful person you admire started unready. The difference is, they didn't let that stop them.

So how do you break out of the learning loop?

Start with execution bias. Don't read another chapter—build something from the last one. Don't watch five videos—apply one idea from the first. Don't buy the toolkit—use the tools already in your garage. Let action lead and let learning trail behind it.

Set limits. Give yourself a 48-hour rule. No more than two days in research mode before you begin doing. Deadlines kill delay.

And most of all, return to why you wanted to learn in the first place. Not to master theory—but to build something real. Learning was never the point. Movement was. And still is.

If this chapter stung a little, that's good. That means it hit something true. Maybe you've been stuck—book to book, podcast to podcast, course to course. Maybe it's time to ask the only question that matters:

What am I actually doing with all this knowledge? If the answer is "not much," don't panic—but don't lie to yourself either. Cut the cord, stop waiting for readiness, stop trying to perfect the map, and start, because the real learning is waiting on the other side.

Chapter 15 — Entropy Is the Enemy

There's a force in the universe that works against order, structure, and forward motion. It doesn't shout or sabotage; it dissolves things slowly. In physics, that force is entropy, the measure of disorder inside a system. According to the Second Law of Thermodynamics, entropy always increases in a closed system. That's what $E > 0$ means: entropy is never zero, never neutral, never resting. It is always rising unless something counteracts it. A room gets messy if you ignore it, metal corrodes on its own, heat spreads out without effort, and clarity becomes fog when left unattended. The drift toward disorder is the natural state of everything, not the exception.

This law applies far beyond physics. It shows up in health, relationships, skills, businesses, and personal projects. If you stop training, your body weakens. If you stop communicating, relationships drift. If you stop creating, your ideas fade. If a business stops imposing structure, internal clutter grows until it chokes movement. None of this requires malice or mistakes; it's simply entropy doing its job. And this is why starting matters so much. Starting is not motivational posturing—it's the practical method for countering a universal law that pushes against you every day.

Life itself is resistance to entropy. Cells organize; DNA replicates; wounds heal by imposing structure on the chaos. Even sleep is an anti-entropy mechanism: a nightly reset that restores order in systems that can't hold it indefinitely. Humans take this further. We create calendars, companies, markets, and books—all acts of pushing back against drift. But the rule stands: the moment we withdraw effort, entropy begins reclaiming ground. It doesn't wait politely. It advances immediately.

Large systems are especially vulnerable. Bureaucracies grow layers of approvals and paperwork until movement slows to a crawl. Universities expand programs but rarely prune them. Corporations add committees faster than they eliminate them. These aren't just inefficiencies; they are entropy becoming culture. Startups, by contrast, move quickly because they fight entropy daily. Governments feel stagnant because they surrendered to it long ago. Without deliberate motion, any system—personal or organizational—slides toward disorder.

Think of entropy as a river that only flows one direction: downward. The current requires no effort to carry you with it. Progress, however, is upstream. It costs energy, intention, and structure. And the strongest upstream stroke is always the first action you take. You don't need a dramatic gesture. You just need to introduce order where disorder is creeping in. One email clears a bottleneck. One decision revives a stalled project. One walk wakes up a dormant body. One honest conversation reopens a relationship that's been drifting. The actions are small, but their effect is large because they interrupt the drift.

Writers know how quickly entropy takes hold. Skip one day and the book loosens its grip. Skip enough days and the story dissolves entirely. The return becomes harder not because you forgot the plot, but because entropy filled the space you abandoned. Writing one clumsy paragraph, however, reclaims that ground immediately. It reestablishes order. It restarts the fight. You can edit a bad paragraph tomorrow; you can't edit a blank one. $E > 0$ explains why even minimal motion has outsized value: it halts the natural slide.

Organizations that thrive build anti-entropy mechanisms into their culture. Amazon's "Day 1" philosophy exists to prevent drift. Toyota's Kaizen exists to counter stagnation with constant small improvements. SpaceX's rapid iteration cycle exists to ensure motion never falls to zero. These companies don't avoid entropy; they acknowledge it and attack it continuously. Burnout often comes not from overwork but from entropy—effort poured into systems that never change, meetings that go nowhere, and cycles that never resolve. The fatigue comes not from motion, but from the absence of it.

Entropy is always rising—that's the physics—and the antidote is always the same: start, not perfectly or dramatically, just enough to interrupt the drift. When you take even a small action, you impose structure on a system that naturally wants to collapse into disorder, reclaiming territory, slowing the current, and over time bending entropy rather than just resisting it. $E > 0$ doesn't mean you're losing; it means the enemy is always present, and starting is how you fight back.

Chapter 16 — Outcome Immunity: The Freedom That Fuels the Start

Most people don't start because they're too focused on how it's going to end. They imagine the pitch going wrong, the video flopping, the call ending in silence, the listing sitting cold, the world saying, "No thanks." So they hesitate. They tweak. They plan more. They hide behind visualization, pretending that imagining the outcome is the same as earning it. But the truth is simple: the mind can't start freely when it's tangled in the outcome.

The best starts come from a different place—a detached place, a clear place. Outcome immunity isn't about indifference. It isn't laziness or the fake-cool shrug of "whatever happens, happens." It's deeper than that. Outcome immunity means you care about the work but don't need the applause. You care about the truth but don't need the sale. You care about showing up but don't need to win. That's when you become dangerous in the best way, because you're no longer fragile, no longer calculating, no longer hinging your worth on a reaction you can't control. You're free.

When you think back on the best conversations, pitches, or interviews you've ever had, they usually happened when you were a little looser, a little lighter, carrying the energy of "I'm here, take it or leave it, I'm good either way." That's not arrogance—it's alignment. And people feel it immediately because you're not clutching at them. You're present instead of preoccupied.

Outcome obsession kills performance. If you've ever frozen in a pitch or stiffened on camera, it wasn't because you lacked knowledge. It was because you were split in two—one half executing, the other half obsessing over how it would be received. That split is death. Overpreparation often makes this worse. You second-guess your tone, your timing, your posture, tweaking as you speak, tightening your rhythm until you sound mechanical. The other side can feel it, and they disengage.

Great performers don't escape this by brute force. They do it by tuning in deeper, by trusting presence. Comedians know this better than anyone. They don't succeed by memorizing every word perfectly. They succeed by reading the room, letting timing and energy guide them, responding in real time. The risk makes it feel alive, and that's why it works. They aren't performing for a scoreboard. They're performing for the moment.

This same truth hides in the sales idea of "go for no." On the surface it's clever: aim for rejections so you build resilience. But the deeper power is that it kills attachment. When you stop chasing yes, your voice loosens up, your tone gets real, your pitch flows naturally. "Go for no" is just outcome immunity in disguise.

Athletes understand this too. A basketball player at the free-throw line isn't visualizing the championship parade. He's breathing, keeping his hands loose, finding rhythm. The moment he shifts from flow to outcome, he chokes. The same goes for tennis players, golfers, or anyone performing under pressure. The ones who thrive don't think harder. They let go harder. They play the moment, not the what-if.

The paradox of outcome immunity is that the moment you

stop needing it, your energy becomes magnetic. People sense the absence of desperation. Conversations open up. Opportunities fall into place. Wins come more often precisely because you weren't hunting them. The loosest grip holds the strongest.

To perform better, you don't need another script, another coaching session, or another deep dive into limiting beliefs. You need to cut the cord between what you do and what it means about you. Let go of how it ends, and the beginning becomes powerful. That's what elite performers understand. Letting go isn't soft. It's lethal.

You can make this practical. Before starting anything high-stakes, pause and reset. Take a breath. Remind yourself: "I'm not here for a yes. I'm here for the truth. No outcome defines me. The doing is enough." Then act without clinging, without calculation. The world doesn't need another desperate pitch. It needs presence.

Outcome immunity isn't apathy. It's clarity. It's what frees you to start. And in the end, that freedom is what wins anyway.

Chapter 17 — Perfection Is the Delay Mechanism

No one wants to admit they're afraid. So they say they're not ready. They say they're still editing, still researching, still tweaking the logo, still building the plan. It sounds responsible, even mature. It can even earn praise. But underneath it all, it isn't discipline and it isn't excellence. It's fear—dressed in better clothes. Perfectionism is just procrastination in a suit and tie.

It feels smart. It feels safe. But it kills motion. The lie of perfection is that it buys you time. What it really buys is distance—distance from the release, the pitch, the publish button, the phone call, the launch. People think they're preparing, but they're stalling.

The moment you say, "I'll just clean it up a little more before I share it," you start slipping. Because now you've told your brain, "Not yet. The moment still isn't safe. Don't show this. You might get hurt." And that's when your system starts treating release as a threat. The longer you delay, the heavier the act of starting becomes.

High performers are especially vulnerable here. They're addicted to control. They want the launch perfect, the pitch bulletproof, the post untouchable. So they stall under the name of craft. They get so deep in the weeds they forget the sunlight is up there. That's why you see people spiral—authors on a third draft for five years, entrepreneurs with fifteen versions of a website and no live offer, salespeople rehearsing calls they'll never make.

The polish is not the problem. The pause is. There's nothing wrong with making something clean and sharp. The danger is when refining becomes hiding. You can usually tell. One more edit feels healthy. Ten more feels like fear. Every new tweak is just your ego trying to control the reaction instead of trusting the movement.

Delay doesn't just slow you down. It rewires you. You stop associating action with reward and start associating it with risk. That's how people freeze. They become planners, upgraders, strategists—everything except starters. They're always "working on something," but never stepping into the ring.

I learned this lesson with drones. When I first started flying, this was before obstacle avoidance was common. I chased a sunset shot one evening, stretching the range, trying to hold the perfect angle. Then the signal drifted and the drone went into the tree line. I recovered it, scratched and scuffed, but it stung. It happened more than once—two drones lost to treetops before I got my rhythm. Painful, but each time I brought them back, I learned something. And in between those crashes, I captured some of the best footage I've ever shot. People still mention those clips today. I didn't get good at flying because I studied every manual or waited until I was flawless. I got good because I flew, crashed, recovered, and flew again.

That's how mastery works. Top performers aren't polished because they're perfectionists. They're polished because they move so often that sharpness is inevitable. The refinement comes from pressure, not pause. You want to write cleaner? Post every day. You want to sell better? Pitch every day. You want to sound natural on camera? Record every day. Perfection doesn't build polish. Repetition does.

And here's the deeper truth—perfection doesn't build trust anyway. People don't want flawless. They want real. They want rhythm, presence, and confidence. A stumble owned in stride builds more trust than a scripted performance. Perfection makes people nervous. Presence makes people relax. Every time you tweak and delay, you're trying to control how people see you instead of trusting them to respond to who you really are.

The perfection loop looks like this: you feel nervous, so you stall. The stall makes you feel behind. That pressure convinces you it has to be better, so you tweak again. And again. Eventually you say, "Not yet." Repeat that twenty times and now your brain can't move forward without fear. You've taught yourself to stall as the default. The only way to break it is to move first.

The truth is, you have to start before you're ready. You have to send before you're sure. You have to launch while it still feels incomplete. That isn't recklessness. That's courage. It's the only way forward motion happens. If you want to beat perfection, set a real deadline and stick to it. Not a soft one you can push. A real one. When the clock hits, you publish. You send. You launch. You move.

Some of the sloppiest things I've ever put out have hit the hardest. I've had raw emails outperform polished campaigns. I've had short, unedited videos get more traction than the ones I planned. I've had conversations land best when I didn't rehearse at all. Why? Because I wasn't trying to impress. I was just moving. Motion creates signal. Perfection delays it.

The principle is simple: perfect is the enemy of present.

Refinement only matters if it still leads to release. Excellence doesn't precede action—it emerges from it. You can't edit your way into trust. You can't plan your way into results. You start. You sharpen. You start again.

The world doesn't reward perfect. It rewards real. It rewards fast. It rewards the person who shows up. Every second you polish past the window, you're burning opportunity. So the only move left is the one you've been avoiding: start anyway. The rest will follow.

Chapter 18 — The Jerk Principle — Restarting With Force

Acceleration isn't the end. It's not even the peak. It's just the second derivative. Beyond acceleration there's another layer, one most people never touch because they never get that far. Physicists call it jerk—the rate of change of acceleration. Not motion. Not speed. Not even momentum. It's what happens when acceleration itself shifts violently, rapidly, without apology. You don't see it. You feel it.

It's the sudden force spike when you launch. The second-stage push. The snap when a system already in motion hits another level of power. And nothing captures this better than a rocket leaving Earth. People imagine rockets as one clean blast upward. They're not. They jerk the entire way. As the engines ignite, acceleration begins—but it doesn't stay steady. The rocket is climbing while burning off mass, fighting gravity, pushing through max air resistance, and shedding stages. None of those transitions are smooth. Each shift in thrust or weight alters the acceleration curve. That's jerk in its rawest form. It doesn't feel like progress—it feels like stress, vibration, and violence.

That's exactly what real breakthroughs feel like. It's never one clean start. It's dozens of micro-surges within a climb. And the higher you go, the more resistance you face. The rocket doesn't wait for the resistance to pass; it jerks harder until it breaks free. That's the metaphor: you don't just start once. You start again inside motion. You accelerate harder while already accelerating.

Most people think starting is going from zero to one, but the deeper start comes midstream. It's when momentum fades and, instead of coasting, you double down. You fire harder exactly where you are. That's how rockets break orbit, and it's how people break plateaus.

Watch Usain Bolt in the 100-meter final at the 2009 World Championships in Berlin. He didn't just accelerate—everyone accelerates at the start. What made that race historic was what happened *after* he was already at top speed. Around 60 meters, when most sprinters begin to fade into the plateau phase, Bolt unleashed something different: a clean spike of force inside full flight. A true jerk. His stride didn't lengthen—his *force output* did. You can see it on the slow-motion analysis: a new layer of power stacked on top of max velocity. That's why the gap opened like a trapdoor. He wasn't maintaining speed; he was adding a new derivative of speed. That's jerk in pure, biological form — acceleration snapping into a higher order.

Or take Game 5 of the 1997 NBA Finals. Michael Jordan, visibly sick, was barely standing, yet he poured in 38 points against the Utah Jazz. Fourth quarter. Tie game. Finals on the line. Exhausted, he still found another surge. Already sprinting, already depleted, he jerked again. That night didn't just win a game—it showed what second-stage force looks like when the tank is empty.

This principle applies everywhere. Writers know it: when you've already been writing and push through resistance, you suddenly hit clarity. Entrepreneurs know it: the first launch is tough, but the later launches—when real pressure mounts—demand new energy injected mid-flight. Sprinters know it: those first awkward, explosive steps out of the blocks are jerky and violent, but they compound into speed.

Jerk is unnatural. Your body resists it; your brain argues against it. Every system in you wants a pause. But if you can fire again when you're already tired, you unlock a zone most never enter—second-stage force. The rocket doesn't stop to regroup when resistance spikes; it adapts by surging harder. That's the only way to break atmosphere.

And that's the truth about growth. It isn't a smooth curve—it's jagged surges of force. Winners aren't just the ones who start; they're the ones who restart inside the climb. They accelerate inside acceleration. They don't plateau and coast. They hit stage two, then stage three, then light solid boosters when most people throttle back.

This isn't reinvention—it's intensified continuation. Jerk doesn't change your direction; it magnifies your trajectory. It's not about a new path; it's about new force on the path you're already on. Which means you don't wait for clarity, you don't wait for stillness, you don't wait to regroup. You hit it again now, while the engines are hot.

Most people plateau at acceleration and call it mastery. But jerk is the real breakthrough zone. And if you're already moving, you're closer than you think. The question isn't whether you can start—it's whether you can surge again when you least feel like it. That's how you leave Earth. That's how you build escape velocity. That's how you change.

Chapter 19 — Don't Brand It, Begin It

Branding is seductive. It makes you feel productive, like you're making progress, when in reality you may just be decorating an idea that hasn't been built yet. Logos, fonts, color schemes, taglines, Instagram grids—these things feel like work, but they're often avoidance. Branding feels like action, but it's really a mask. You're preparing to prepare.

The danger is that branding promises clarity but delivers delay. It shifts the focus from presence to packaging, from impact to image. It convinces creators that the way something looks is more important than whether it actually exists. Why do we fall for it? Because branding is controlled, clean, and safe. Starting something real is messy. It opens you up to judgment. It demands stakes. Branding lets you hide in the shallow end. You can look busy without ever taking the risk of beginning.

Psychologists call this kind of avoidance precrastination—the tendency to jump on easy, surface-level tasks to postpone harder, more meaningful ones. A 2014 study from Penn State showed that people prefer to check off simple boxes, even if it makes the harder work take longer. Branding is the ultimate version of this. You feel forward momentum while your actual work waits. A 2021 paper in the Journal of Consumer Psychology backed this up: entrepreneurs who spent early energy on logos and design were significantly less likely to follow through on their projects. The dopamine of early branding tricked them into feeling progress they hadn't earned.

The lesson is everywhere. Tropicana learned it the hard way in 2009 when they rebranded their packaging and sales dropped 20% in two months, costing them $50 million. They had obsessed over design and ignored clarity. Consumers didn't recognize the product. Branding, instead of helping, killed the business momentum. The truth is simple: aesthetics can never compensate for a lack of real work.

History is full of examples that prove the opposite. Phil Knight started what became Nike by selling running shoes out of his car. There was no swoosh, no "Just Do It," no brand campaigns—just product, motion, and conversations with real runners. Google, Spotify, Yahoo, Häagen-Dazs—all these names sounded odd or meaningless in the beginning. They only became iconic because the work behind them delivered. A brand is a shadow. The body is the work.

Substance always beats aesthetic. Kodak poured millions into branding campaigns while its core product lagged. They collapsed anyway. Airbnb started with a clunky website, air mattresses, and cereal-box gimmicks to stay afloat. Nobody cared about their logo. People cared that the service worked. Identity followed results.

The temptation to polish your presence is strong, but it's misplaced. Your Instagram feed is not your business. Your bio is not your value. Branding might eventually help once you have something to refine, but in the beginning it's a distraction. Real brands are built on trust, consistency, and delivery. They are built one solved problem at a time.

I knew a woman who spent two years preparing to launch her podcast. She designed logos, bought equipment, and fussed over names. One day she finally said, "Forget it," recorded a twelve-minute episode on Voice Memos, and uploaded it raw. That show is now a top-50 podcast in her niche. Her logo is still average. Her name is still odd. None of it mattered. What mattered was that she started.

The pattern repeats everywhere. The coffee cart with no name and no signage that grew into a full shop. The writer who built an audience before ever thinking about design. The local creator who focused on showing up rather than polishing their identity. They all understood the truth: people don't care what you look like until they care what you do.

That's the point. Branding can help once there's something real to shape, but until then it's just a shadow. You can't chase the shadow. You have to build the body. The only way to do that is to begin.

So stop asking, "What should my brand be?" Ask, "What am I doing today that helps someone?" Ask, "What problem am I solving?" Ask, "Where can I get feedback?" Those answers will create your brand. Not a color palette.

The world doesn't need another polished logo floating on an empty promise. It needs people willing to build, to deliver, to begin. Don't brand it. Begin it. Do the work first. Refine later. Let your brand emerge as proof that you showed up, not as decoration for a dream.

PART III — Tools of the Start

Chapter 20 — First Steps That Changed the World

History doesn't remember the planners. It remembers the starters. We glorify the achievements, the headlines, the IPOs, and the books written after the fact. But behind every leap forward—every movement, every business, every cultural shift—there was a first step. And that step usually wasn't clean. It wasn't glamorous. It was awkward, untested, and full of doubt. But it mattered more than everything that came after.

It's easy to romanticize what happens later: the breakthrough product, the stadium rally, the world-changing speech. But none of that exists without the first imperfect step, usually taken quietly and often alone. That's how revolutions begin. That's how entire industries are born. That's how lives change—one bold move forward when the conditions are not yet right.

Rosa Parks gave us one of the clearest examples of this truth. The civil rights movement was already in motion in 1955, but when she refused to give up her seat on that Montgomery bus, the movement surged into a new gear. Her act wasn't scripted or grand. It was a simple no. And that first step of resistance—ordinary in the moment, monumental in hindsight—helped ignite one of the most powerful social shifts in American history. She wasn't trying to become an icon. She was tired. She acted. That's what real first steps look like. They don't feel epic at the time.

The Wright brothers knew the same reality. In 1903, in the sand dunes of Kitty Hawk, Orville and Wilbur weren't certain their machine would fly. They weren't even sure it would stay intact. They had no guarantees, no endorsements, no blueprint to follow. But they took the step. They built, they tested, they launched. That fragile 12-second flight changed history—not because it was long, but because it happened. Their first step didn't look like mastery. It looked like wobbling just above the ground. But that wobble became aviation.

Steve Jobs and Steve Wozniak's garage experiment worked the same way. Before Apple transformed the world with the iPhone, before personal computers became part of every household, there was a crude, hand-assembled prototype built in obscurity. Nobody asked for it. Nobody was waiting. There was no demand and no audience. There was just curiosity and a decision to act. Their first step was a box of circuits that looked nothing like the sleek devices that came later. But that first step—messy and uncertain—was the beginning of a revolution.

The pattern repeats in every arena. People want to wait for clarity, for certainty, for some sign that the risk will pay off. But history belongs to those who move without guarantees. Psychologists call it behavioral momentum: once something is in motion, it becomes harder to stop. Even a tiny first step creates the feedback loop needed for progress. Action releases dopamine. It reshapes identity. It turns you from an observer into a participant. And once you're in motion, the path reveals itself.

Research supports this. In 2017, a study from the University of Zurich tracked hundreds of early-stage entrepreneurs. Those who launched even a rough version of their idea within 30 days were three times more likely to reach profitability within two years compared to those who kept planning. It wasn't the quality of the first step that made the difference. It was the existence of it. The starters got feedback faster, adapted faster, and built resilience faster. The planners stayed safe, but they also stayed stuck.

We tell ourselves we're being responsible when we wait. That we're preparing. That we're setting the stage for a better launch later. But most of the time, waiting is just fear in disguise. We're afraid to look foolish. Afraid to fail publicly. Afraid that the outcome will confirm our doubts. But what if none of that matters? What if the only thing that matters is that the first step exists at all?

Every first step looks small on the outside. But on the inside, it's a seismic shift. It changes how you see yourself. You go from spectator to participant. From dreamer to doer. From someone with an idea to someone with momentum. And that shift compounds into everything that comes next.

It's tempting to think you're too late—that others have already started, already succeeded, already claimed the space. But every single person who is ahead of you once stood where you are now, staring down the same fear, unsure if the next move mattered. The truth is, there is no expiration date on courage. There is no penalty for starting late. There is only a penalty for not starting at all.

The Wright brothers, Rosa Parks, Steve Jobs—they didn't wait for perfect conditions. They didn't know their steps would change the world. They just moved. That's the real difference. Not brilliance. Not certainty. Not flawless timing. Just action.

First steps are never perfect. They are rarely impressive. But they are always the most important move you will ever make. Because without them, nothing else happens. And with them, everything becomes possible.

Chapter 21 — The One Brick Rule

Everyone wants to build something. A business. A career. A body of work. A reputation. A legacy. But when you stare at the whole thing, it feels impossible. The vision is exciting until it paralyzes you. That's when the mind floods with doubt—"It's too much. I'll never get there. What's the point of even trying?" This is where the One Brick Rule saves you. Forget the mansion. Just lay one brick. You don't need to build the whole wall today. You don't need to climb the mountain in one sprint. All you need to do is place the next brick with care, with presence, with whatever skill you can give in that moment. It's the simplest rule in the world: one brick, well placed, every day.

Humans aren't built to carry the weight of big, abstract goals. We burn out under the pressure. We choke under vast expectations. But we are excellent at handling simple, specific tasks. When you shift from "I have to build something huge" to "I'm just laying one brick today," the pressure drops. The brain locks in. It can move. Momentum builds because the scope shrinks. Every time you lay a brick, your nervous system gets a small hit of satisfaction—not because the job is done, but because something is real now. You've changed the shape of the world.

Elite athletes live by this rule, whether they call it that or not. They don't obsess about championships in every workout. They focus on today's drill, this morning's lift, or that single backhand slice. Tiger Woods once practiced the same chip shot hundreds of times, not because it was glamorous, but because it was foundational. One shot, one motion, one brick. Stack enough bricks like that, and what looks like genius is actually repetition, investment, and presence.

This rule beats the all-or-nothing trap that derails so many people. Too often, we swing for big moves, hoping one miracle play will change everything. But big moves without a base collapse fast. What works is the quiet compounding of effort. Every brick you lay makes the next one easier. It builds rhythm, feedback, and confidence. You don't need a miracle. You need to keep stacking.

Research backs this up. A study at the University of Chicago showed that when people faced large, open-ended goals, their cognitive performance dropped—working memory, decision-making, and even emotional stability suffered. But when those same goals were broken into small, task-based chunks, performance improved. The brain doesn't respond to scale. It responds to specificity. "Write a book" overwhelms. "Write 200 words" activates. "Get in shape" paralyzes. "Do 25 push-ups" mobilizes. One brick.

The brick also has shape. One mistake people make is thinking that showing up is enough. But the One Brick Rule isn't about being busy. It's about being deliberate. Reaching out to one client instead of scrolling Zillow for hours. Writing one clean paragraph instead of sketching ten half-done ideas. Cleaning one corner of the garage instead of watching four organization videos. The brick has intent. It doesn't need to be big, but it must be real.

When you meet someone who's built something substantial—a thriving business, a long marriage, a body of work—they'll often tell you some version of the same story: "I just kept showing up. I did the next thing. Then the next. Then the next." That's the One Brick Rule. Most people don't quit because they're incapable. They quit because they tried to lay the entire wall at once. When it wobbled, they bailed. When it didn't look impressive by day four, they thought they failed. The ones who stay, the ones who trust the bricks, outlast everyone.

For me, the brick is writing. I don't try to finish a chapter in a day. I just aim for one strong section, one clear passage. I open the document, find the next empty space, and put something true into it. Sometimes I hate what I write. Sometimes I love it. But every day, I place a brick. And now I've got a wall. This book wasn't built with a master plan. It was built with bricks.

You don't owe the world a masterpiece. You don't owe anyone a perfect launch, a flawless streak, or a brilliant week. You owe the process one brick today. Put it down. Step back. Let it settle. Then come back tomorrow and place another. One brick, well placed, every day. That's the rule, and it works.

Of course, you'll miss a day. Maybe two. Maybe more. And the mind will whisper, "You blew it. You're off schedule. You'll never catch up." Ignore it. The One Brick Rule doesn't care how many you missed. It only cares about the next one. You don't owe the pile anything. You don't need to backfill a wall. You only need to place the next brick. Think of this rule as forward only—no guilt, no debt, just action. Progress isn't about being perfect. It's about being consistent enough to keep stacking.

Every brick is a vote for the kind of person you're becoming. When you choose to lay one brick—no matter how small—you tell your future self, "I'm someone who builds. I'm someone who keeps going. I'm someone who values today." That identity isn't formed in motivational peaks. It's built in quiet, deliberate acts that no one sees. One day, you'll look up and realize you've built something lasting. Something real. And it all started because you placed one brick and didn't stop. That's the whole game.

Chapter 22 — The Magic of Showing Up

In every arena—business, sports, relationships, and life—the winners aren't always the most talented. They're the ones who keep showing up. They do it when it's boring, when it's awkward, when it's unclear, when it's raining. They show up when they're tired, when they're unsure, when no one else does. There's a quiet power in this. Not the lightning bolt kind of magic, but the kind you earn over time.

Keep showing up, and things begin to shift. Not because the world bends instantly to your effort, but because consistency creates gravity. You start to attract people, clarity, and momentum—not with brilliance, but with presence. You stop waiting for luck. You become the kind of person luck finds.

Showing up doesn't mean going through the motions. It means being where your feet are. Fully. It means engaging even when the outcome isn't guaranteed. It means doing the reps not because you're inspired, but because that's who you are now. There's a difference between attendance and engagement. The effect only compounds when you're truly engaged, not just present in body, but present in focus.

Most people misunderstand consistency. They think it's about grind and brute force. It's not. It's about presence—mental and physical. One hour of real presence beats five hours of distracted effort. You've seen this in meetings, in training sessions, in creative work: the person who's all-in for thirty minutes does more than the one who multitasks for three.

The student who shows up to study group, even when they feel behind, is on the right track. The new agent who walks into the office early, even with no clients, is building something. The writer who opens the document every morning, even when the words won't come, is already ahead. You don't need to crush the day. You need to keep the pattern alive.

Showing up builds credibility—not just with the world, but with yourself. Each time you show up, you reinforce identity. You become more of the person you say you are. Over time, that identity becomes difficult to break.

A study at Columbia University in 2010 tracked students with similar SAT scores and GPAs across various programs. The strongest predictor of success wasn't intelligence or participation. It was attendance. Just being there correlated with better comprehension, higher retention, and greater graduation rates. Presence created pattern, and pattern created learning. Learning became momentum, and momentum became confidence. It all began with showing up.

Woody Allen once joked that eighty percent of success is just showing up. It sounds like a throwaway line, but there's truth in it. You can't win the audition, land the client, or close the deal if you're not in the room. Most people eliminate themselves before the first round. They wait for the perfect moment or the perfect plan. That moment never comes. The person who showed up—half-prepared but fully present—gets the chance they didn't.

We overestimate the importance of being amazing and underestimate the value of being there. You don't have to be great to start. You just have to start to be great. And that begins with showing up.

The problem isn't day one. Starting is exciting. It's also not day two or three. The real test comes in the middle days. That's when motivation wears off, the novelty fades, and no one is clapping. This is when most people fall off. Not with a big declaration, but by quietly opting out. They simply stop showing up.

The ones who keep going in those middle days—the quiet, unsexy, unrewarded ones—are the ones who gain the compounding effect. Presence stacks. People may not remember every single action you took, but they will feel the weight of your consistency. Reputations aren't built on peaks. They're built on what you do when no one is watching.

The brain responds to presence, too. A 2016 study at Duke University found that regular engagement—even low-effort engagement—in problem-solving tasks improved both cognitive flexibility and stress resilience. Showing up rewired the brain to see challenges as manageable instead of threatening. In practical terms, this meant the brain learned to stay calm when others froze. What feels impossible today becomes routine six months from now—if you keep showing up.

Of course, there will be days you don't want to. Days you feel invisible, ineffective, or stuck. That's when showing up matters most. You're not showing up because it guarantees success. You're showing up because it preserves direction. Momentum is fragile. Skip long enough and it's hard to return. Even one small step keeps the pattern alive.

There's a saying in the military: stay in the fight. That's what showing up is. You don't have to dominate every round. You just have to refuse to leave the ring. Eventually the tide turns, but it can't turn if you're not there to see it.

Think of the teacher who opens the classroom early every morning, even when students don't arrive until later. Parents notice. Students notice. Administrators notice. They may not comment on it, but it becomes a pattern—and patterns build trust. Or the young professional who logs into every meeting two minutes early, even when nothing is discussed. People begin to associate them with reliability. They get called on. They get trusted. Not because they're the smartest, but because they're there.

That's the compounding effect of showing up. You don't need a breakthrough every time. You don't need applause or proof. You just need to be in the room, doing the work. You're not chasing perfection. You're building trust—with others and with yourself.

The deal that changes everything? You only get it because you kept showing up when nothing was happening. The client who finally calls? They remembered you because you didn't disappear. The opportunity that looked like luck? It landed on your desk because you were still at the desk.

Showing up makes you lucky because it puts you in more rooms, around more people, with more chances to be seen, chosen, hired, or trusted, and over time those chances compound, stack, and multiply. Show up long enough and the results will come, because the world rewards consistency more than it rewards brilliance.

Chapter 23 — Starting Makes You Smarter

You've heard the phrase "knowledge is power." But in the real world, knowledge without action is just trivia. Power comes when knowledge collides with movement. The person who starts—who moves—gains real intelligence. Not just surface experience, but deeper cognitive sharpness. The mind literally rewires itself in response to action.

Starting activates pattern recognition. It sharpens memory. It turns abstract concepts into lived understanding. The brain learns best in motion, and starting is the trigger. This isn't motivational fluff—it's neuroscience.

In 2014, researchers at the University of Illinois described what they called "embodied cognition." Their finding was simple: the brain doesn't just absorb information passively, it's shaped by what the body does. Write one paragraph and you learn more than reading ten. Swing a golf club and you internalize more than watching twenty tutorials. The instant you start doing, your brain shifts from analyzing to adapting. That shift—from watcher to mover—puts the brain in a higher gear.

This is why beginners often improve faster than experts. They're not protecting status or clinging to theory. They're failing, adjusting, and learning. Meanwhile, the expert can get stuck in preservation mode, avoiding risks that would actually sharpen them.

Most people wait for readiness before they start. But readiness is a mirage. Learning doesn't double before action, it doubles because of action. Think about trying to learn a language. You can memorize vocabulary for months, but nothing rewires your brain like ordering food in another country. The pressure flips the brain into problem-solving mode. It rewires on the fly.

The same is true in business, sports, or creative work. Questions become sharper, memory sticks better, and priorities become clear. Action filters what matters. Without it, everything in your head feels equally important, which is why overthinkers stall.

At Stanford, a long-term study of first-year engineering students found that those who built prototypes immediately—rather than endlessly sketching and theorizing—scored higher in innovation, retention, and collaboration. The devices they made weren't always better, but their thinking was. The act of building sharpened cognition more than talking about building ever could.

The mechanism is plasticity—the brain's ability to rewire itself. But plasticity doesn't respond to perfection. It responds to friction, novelty, and challenge. Start something just beyond your skill level and your brain lights up. It tries to create new maps, new pathways, new solutions. Sit too long in planning mode and that opportunity dulls.

Real intelligence comes from decisions, not delay. Intelligence is pattern recognition, and patterns only appear through exposure. You can't recognize a sales trend without talking to buyers. You can't get better at closing without pitching. You can't refine writing without publishing. Each attempt, even a wrong one, sharpens your instincts.

That's why entrepreneurs often build better second companies.

They move faster, cut dead weight sooner, and test ideas with less ego. Their edge isn't from theory—it's from starts.

The science backs this up. A 2018 study at the Max Planck Institute showed that participants who acted on problems early—even before fully understanding them—activated the dorsolateral prefrontal cortex, the brain's hub for executive function and decision-making. They retained knowledge longer and performed better because their learning was tied to urgency and context, not passive review.

Practical intelligence—the kind psychologist Robert Sternberg described—comes only from this. It's the intelligence of navigating conflict, prioritizing under pressure, reading a room. You can't absorb it. You can only earn it by moving.

Overthinking is not intelligence. It's unused potential. Starting gives the brain a filter. It discards noise, highlights relevance, and builds clarity. Each imperfect decision makes you sharper.

This isn't about working harder. It's about activating a different gear in the mind. Starting flips the switch. It moves you from passive to active, from theory to practice, from hoping to adjusting. And in that shift, intelligence compounds.

So don't wait for clarity, permission, or readiness—start, and let your mind catch up. Every level you've ever reached in life began with that sequence: you moved first, and your brain got smarter because of it.

Chapter 24 — The Countdown Hack — Winning the War on Small Tasks

There's a special kind of failure that doesn't feel like failure. It's not the big missed opportunity or the dramatic collapse. It's the slow, grinding drag of neglected small tasks—tiny actions that rot in the corners of your day. The sock never picked up. The empty fridge that stays empty. The three dishes in the sink that somehow multiply into twenty. It's not hard. It's just unstarted.

These are the silent killers of momentum—the anti-starts. They don't break you all at once. They steal time, compound inertia, and inject friction into your routine until everything feels heavier than it really is. Small tasks unstarted are large tasks waiting to ambush you. They don't stay small. They metastasize. And they hijack your bandwidth every time you walk past them without doing them.

But what if you could dismantle them without brute force? What if the key wasn't willpower or discipline—but curiosity?

The hack is almost embarrassingly simple: count. Out loud or silently. Just count. Count to yourself as you do the task. One… two… three… You're not counting down like a rocket launch—you're counting up like a stopwatch. You're creating a micro-timer, not to race the clock, but to witness the truth of what the task costs.

Here's the surprising part: most of the tasks you avoid take less than 30 seconds. Putting on a belt. Taking the trash out. Throwing a dirty shirt into the hamper. Wiping the counter. Closing six browser tabs. Sending a one-line email. These things don't take long—they just get heavy in your head.

Counting flips the script. It turns the moment into a curiosity experiment. You're not forcing yourself to do something—you're testing how long it takes. That shift—from resistance to observation—kills the lie that these things are "too much right now."

Here's how it works:
You feel resistance.
Instead of fighting it, you start counting.
The moment you count "one," you're already in motion.
And often by "six," the task is done.

That's not motivation. That's momentum. And momentum is resistance's worst enemy.

This isn't magic—it's psychology. The Zeigarnik Effect, discovered in the 1920s, shows that unfinished tasks occupy more mental space than completed ones. The brain loops unfinished business until it's resolved. Even a partial start reduces that tension. Counting breaks overwhelming mental clutter into solvable micro-wins. It also kills task-time distortion, where you overestimate how long something will take. Ten seconds reveals the truth.

The beauty is that curiosity runs smooth. Unlike discipline, which fatigues, curiosity asks a simple, playful question: "How long will this really take?" And that's enough to bypass the stall.

Neglected small tasks don't just clutter your space—they eat your identity. The trash you didn't take out this morning isn't just trash. It's a subconscious cue that you're someone who leaves things undone. That's the real danger. Delay teaches you to see yourself as a procrastinator. Action, even small action, rewrites the identity.

You can even apply this hack to bigger low-friction tasks—running to the store, dropping something off, refilling the gas tank. If you catch yourself hesitating, start counting. "One… two… three…" By the time you're at ten, the shoes are on and the car is started. Inertia is broken. The task is already in motion.

And once one small task falls, others usually follow. This is task chaining. You put away a dish, then wipe the counter, then answer that text. You didn't plan to—but your brain is now in start mode.

Look around. What have you been avoiding for two days that takes under thirty seconds? Deleting junk screenshots. Refolding a shirt. Plugging in your phone. Watering a plant. Wiping the toothpaste off the mirror. Start counting. If you're done before fifteen, you've crushed resistance without a fight. If it takes longer, no problem—you've exposed the reality instead of the fear.

The biggest lie in the room is, "I don't have time." When you count through your tasks, you discover that time isn't the issue. Friction is. Anticipation is. It's not resistance to finishing—it's resistance to starting.

Every time you count, you remind yourself that you don't need to feel like it or want it—you just need to see what it takes, and usually it takes less than ten seconds. That's the countdown hack: ten seconds to pick up momentum, ten seconds to break resistance, ten seconds to win the moment, because small starts aren't small at all—they're the hidden levers that shift entire days, and when you add them up, they don't just clean the sink or empty the trash, they build a habit of starting, and that habit is how you win.

Chapter 25 — Start Before the Vision Is Clear

Most people wait for clarity. They convince themselves that once the vision sharpens, once the map becomes legible, once the path lights up—they'll move. They think the right answer will click into place like a puzzle piece, and when it does, then they'll finally act. But it doesn't work that way. Vision doesn't show up before the action. It arrives in pieces, through motion, through friction, through the dull repetition of showing up in uncertainty. Waiting for certainty is the most seductive form of self-sabotage there is. It wears the mask of wisdom. It presents as maturity. It says, "Don't rush. Think it through." But underneath it, if we're honest, is fear. Fear of waste. Fear of embarrassment. Fear of being wrong. So we stall under the guise of strategy.

The truth is that most people who make something real don't start with a vision—they start with a pull. A small compulsion. A gut-level nudge. Not a detailed plan. Not a full-blown mission. Just an impulse they honor before it makes total sense. They begin while the picture is blurry. The vision doesn't become clear first—it gets clear because they began. Every builder, artist, entrepreneur, leader, preacher, and parent worth anything started in fog. Michelangelo once said he saw the angel in the marble and carved until he set him free, but that's poetic hindsight. At the beginning, he just had a block of stone. A hard, cold, heavy chunk. The angel wasn't obvious. The lines weren't mapped. But he began chipping anyway. Not because he knew exactly what he was making, but because not carving wasn't an option. That's how you make anything real. You don't wait for the angel to appear—you start swinging the hammer.

86

People like to tell themselves that the greats had it all figured out before they took their shot. That they had the whole plan mapped, the pitch ready, the vision dialed. They didn't. They just started better. They knew that waiting for a complete picture was a fantasy. They knew the only way forward was to take the next step, even if it felt dumb or premature. You don't need a blueprint—you need a brick. You don't need a business plan—you need a sale. You don't need a map—you need momentum. In every meaningful pursuit, the vision is earned through action. It sharpens with every rep, every mistake, every course correction. The fog doesn't clear from a distance—it lifts as you walk into it.

I've watched people lose years of their lives because they thought they needed to plan more before acting. I've seen founders stall out building pitch decks while someone else launched a rough first version and stole the market. I've watched would-be authors map out perfect outlines but never write a single word. I've seen personal projects, relationships, and businesses die in the womb because the person waited for the green light that never came. The brutal truth is this: iteration beats imagination. Clarity, like confidence, is something you build—not something you wait for.

People always talk about timing, but they forget that timing isn't about perfection—it's about proximity. The closer you get to the thing, the more it reveals itself. But you don't earn that proximity from the sidelines. You earn it by starting messy, starting scared, starting wrong. It's not that clarity gives you courage. It's that courage gives you clarity. Want a better picture of your future? Start moving toward it. Want to know what you really want? Start doing something—anything—and watch how quickly the real answers surface.

Some of the best things in your life happened before you were ready. You didn't plan your way into them—you stumbled into them, responded to them, said yes to them in the middle of the fog. You didn't wait for the full picture. You stepped in with partial vision. The big wins don't come from careful timing. They come from bold presence. Showing up while the map is still being drawn. Starting before the vision is clear isn't a gamble—it's the only way the vision becomes clear at all.

There's research to back this up. A study from NYU and Stanford split participants into two groups: one group was told to spend time crafting a clear vision for a major goal before acting, while the other group was instructed to start small without overthinking the final outcome. The results weren't close. The early-action group reported higher motivation, greater follow-through, and—most interesting—clearer vision than the planning group. The researchers called it "emergent clarity." The people who moved first ended up seeing farther. The ones who waited for vision got stuck. That tells you everything. Clarity isn't a prerequisite—it's a byproduct of movement.

One of the great success stories in South Florida began with a businessman from Argentina who arrived without a blueprint, mentor, or grand vision. He started small—managing a condo building. Nothing glamorous. No headlines. Just solving problems and learning the terrain. From there, he built a boutique real estate business, then took a leap and bought a prime piece of land. That move opened the door to something bigger. One project led to another, and eventually he became a developer, shaping the skyline of Miami with a series of high-rise towers that now define the city. He didn't wait until he had it all figured out. He just kept moving. One step at a time. Forward. Foggy. Uncertain. But always forward. His story isn't about luck or genius—it's about motion. The vision came later. The clarity came because he acted without it.

You've probably seen this in your own life. You begin something you're unsure about—maybe a move, a job, a commitment—and somewhere along the way, you realize it was the right call. But only in hindsight. The clarity wasn't there at the start. You had to walk blind for a while. You had to take hits. You had to adjust. That's the trade. You want vision? Put in the steps. Burn the energy. Pay the price of uncertainty. The ones who make it are not the ones who waited—they're the ones who moved anyway.

If you want to test this for yourself, take one idea you've been avoiding because it "isn't ready." Then do the most embarrassingly small version of it today. Not tomorrow. Today. Record a 30-second voice memo. Write a single paragraph. Send one email. Not because it's good, but because it's movement. Then watch what happens. Your brain starts recalibrating. The fog lifts by a degree. The gears engage. You're in the game. And once you're in, the rest starts to fall into place—not all at once, but enough to keep you going.

The longer you delay, the more the delay becomes the default. And that's the real cost. Not just lost time—but erosion. Entropy. A slow internal decay that teaches your body you don't follow through. And the more you train yourself not to start, the harder starting gets. You lose momentum, sure—but more dangerously, you lose your own credibility. You don't trust your word anymore. And without that trust, everything starts to cost more: emotionally, mentally, spiritually. Starting becomes a kind of rehab. A way back to yourself.

THE MAGIC OF STARTING

You don't need to see the whole staircase. Just the next step. The road reveals itself with each footfall. The map is printed with your footprints. The vision is not the prerequisite—it's the reward.

PART IV — Building Momentum

Chapter 26 — Ignition Over Identity

The self-help industry has spent the last decade obsessed with identity. Books, podcasts, and gurus all chant the same mantra: "You must become the type of person who does the thing." On paper, it sounds profound. In reality, it's a trap.

You don't need a new identity to take action. You need action to build a new identity.

Too many people are waiting for a shift in self-perception before they move. They tell themselves that once they feel like the kind of person who starts a business, writes a book, or gets fit—then they'll act. But that moment never comes. They stall. They consume more content. They prepare endlessly. They don't move.

Years ago, I knew a guy with no pedigree, no degree, no network. He worked odd jobs, scraped by, and had a couple of run-ins with the law. Nobody would have pegged him as a "business guy." But he got a shot working for a property manager in a rough part of Miami—cleaning trash, fixing leaks, hauling appliances. Nothing glamorous.

He showed up anyway. Six days a week. No title, no plan, no identity. Just work.

Two years in, he was managing properties. Not because he rebranded himself, but because he kept solving problems no one else wanted. Then he spotted a cheap duplex. He didn't know the finance side, but he scraped together a loan, bought it, fixed it, rented it. That was ignition.

Fast forward ten years, and he owned several buildings and ran his own development firm. He never journaled affirmations about becoming a real estate mogul. He just moved. And his identity caught up.

That's how it really works. Identity isn't the launchpad. It's the residue of motion.

Psychology backs this up. Daryl Bem's Self-Perception Theory argues that we form beliefs about ourselves by observing our own behavior. You don't feel like a leader and then act like one—you act like a leader, and eventually you believe it.

This is why military training starts with bed-making and drills, not therapy or mindset workshops. Behavior first. Mindset follows. A recruit doesn't "feel disciplined" on day one. They do the reps. Over time, the identity becomes real because it's been earned.

Business works the same way. The ones who win don't wait until they're ready. They launch messy. They stumble through the calls. They take action that feels clumsy and half-baked. And in the doing, they discover who they are becoming.

The ones who lose? They stay stuck in identity-building mode. They want the perfect logo before they make the first sale. They want to feel like entrepreneurs before risking a dollar. They spend their lives "becoming" instead of actually doing.

The chain that works is simple: motion creates feedback. Feedback creates insight. Insight builds improvement. Improvement builds confidence. Confidence shapes identity. But it all begins with ignition.

Want to be a writer? Don't wait until you feel like one. Write. Publish. Take the heat. Then keep writing. Want to sell? Stop reading sales books and start dialing. Want to get in shape? Don't visualize yourself as an athlete. Just sweat.

At first, you'll feel like an outsider. But if you stay in the room—long enough and often enough—you'll stop pretending to belong. You'll just belong. Not because of belief, but because of evidence. You did the work.

We are what we repeatedly do. Identity follows time, effort, and energy—not intention. The man who spends three hours building a business and one hour scrolling social media will view himself differently than the man who does the reverse, no matter what both say out loud.

I've seen addicts become mentors. Waiters turn into restaurant owners. Workers turn into developers. The common thread wasn't mindset shifts or identity affirmations. It was ignition. They acted. They moved. The rest followed.

The era we live in glorifies alignment. But waiting to feel aligned is often a luxury. More often, you act before you feel. And then your emotions fall in line with your effort.

The myth is that successful people start with a strong identity. Most don't. They just have a bias toward action. They'd rather risk being wrong than be stuck. That's why they win ground while others wait.

Identity will lie to you, telling you you're not ready or not that person, but action will prove it wrong. You don't need belief to light the fire; you need the match—ignition first, identity second—and when in doubt, move. You'll trust yourself later because you acted now, and when you finally look back, you'll see the truth: you were never lacking belief, only motion.

Chapter 27 — The Myth of Motion

We're taught to glorify movement. Stay busy. Hustle harder. Fill every hour. It sounds right—especially to high performers. But here's the uncomfortable truth: not all motion is progress. Most motion is just avoidance disguised as work.

There's real movement—the kind that makes money, builds muscle, writes chapters, closes deals. And there's fake movement—tweaking your website for the third time, brainstorming menus, watching sales videos instead of actually selling. Motion looks productive, but it isn't. Activity isn't achievement.

Real progress carries resistance. It's uncomfortable. It has stakes. You can fail. You can get rejected. That's why people avoid it. Instead, they fill their days with motion—safe, low-impact tasks that feel good but change nothing.

When I started at Coldwell Banker, I fell into this trap. I was green, eager, and thought professionalism meant perfection. My files were flawless—organized, tabbed, immaculate. I treated paperwork like the job itself. One day, the office secretary, Ony, complimented me: "James, your files are beautiful. You really take this seriously." I felt proud. Then she added, almost casually: "You're nothing like Pamela."

Pamela was the top producer. Mega listings, nonstop closings. Ony continued, "Pamela's files are a mess. But she doesn't care. She just wants to make money." That was the wake-up call. Pamela wasn't winning because of paperwork. She was winning because she was out in the field, taking risks, making moves.

From then on, I decided: better messy files and full commission checks than perfect paperwork and an empty pipeline. And I've kept that principle ever since.

That's the difference between motion and action. Motion looks tidy. Action produces results.

The myth of motion is believing that doing something is always better than doing nothing. But sometimes doing the wrong thing over and over is worse than standing still—because it convinces you you're making progress. Spinning in neutral feels like movement, but you're going nowhere.

Real action leaves evidence. It moves the scoreboard. It produces outcomes. Fifty cold calls. One closed deal. A published page. A launched ad. A knocked door. That's action.

Motion, on the other hand, is like rocking in a chair—you're busy, but you never leave the porch.

Preparation has its place. You need some planning, some learning, a baseline of skill. But most people cross the line without noticing. They hide in preparation. They live in endless planning. It feels safe, but it's just delay.

Ask yourself: What in your routine feels productive but doesn't actually move the needle? Answer that honestly and you'll see how much of your day is motion—not action.

Motion tricks the brain. It gives you the dopamine hit of problem-solving without the risk. A new planner. A new podcast. A new app. You feel smart, but nothing real has changed.

The ones who win? They act in the spaces that carry risk—where rejection, failure, and discomfort live. Because that's where growth lives too.

Writers who finish books aren't endlessly outlining—they're publishing pages that scare them. Fitness isn't researched, it's trained. Business isn't brainstormed, it's shipped.

That's why professionals separate themselves. They stop performing productivity and start producing.

If you're writing—write.
If you're selling—sell.
If you're building—launch.

Everything else is noise.

Do you want to look busy, or do you want to be effective? Because you can't be both, and the moment you choose action over motion, everything shifts. Results stack, momentum compounds, and you stop living in rehearsal and start living in reality—not because you worked harder, but because you finally worked on the thing that mattered. The myth dies the day you stop hiding in motion and start producing outcomes, and that choice is the one that decides everything.

Chapter 28 — You Don't Have to Like It to Start It

There's a myth we've been sold in almost every productivity book, podcast, and seminar. It's the idea that we need to feel good about a task in order to begin it. That the right mindset, the right music, the right tone or temperature or caffeine balance will somehow make the hard things feel easy. The myth goes like this: once you're in the zone, everything will flow.

But most meaningful work—the kind that changes your life or pays the bills—starts with something else: friction. Especially the kind of work that's necessary but not glamorous. Prospecting. Cold calls. Filling in spreadsheets. Following up. These aren't sexy tasks. They don't give you a dopamine hit just for showing up. And no amount of visualization or playlist tinkering is going to turn them into something they're not.

The real key is knowing how to act when the work feels like a drag. And it starts by understanding what your brain is doing when you're hesitating. The moment you sit down and start thinking about the task—before doing anything at all—a quiet mental machine kicks on in the background. It's called the Default Mode Network, or DMN for short. It's the part of your brain that lights up when you're not engaged with the outside world. When you're daydreaming, reflecting, ruminating, doubting, rehearsing conversations in your head. The DMN is why you feel stuck before you begin. It loops thoughts. It whispers distractions. It creates inner tension that grows the longer you sit idle.

Then something wild happens the moment you start doing.

Not thinking about doing—actually doing. Your brain flips. It shifts into a completely different system called the Task-Positive Network (TPN). This system fires up the circuits that help you focus, execute, solve, and move. The hesitation fog lifts. The self-talk fades. The noise quiets down. And suddenly you're in motion.

Here's the part that matters: your brain can't run both networks at once. They're in competition. If you're lost in your head, DMN is running the show. If you're doing the task—typing the number, starting the list, dialing the call—TPN takes over. The fastest way to win the war is to give TPN a reason to turn on. Start small. Start now. But start.

I remember sitting at my desk one Tuesday morning staring at a single phone number. Just one. A local For Sale By Owner. It wasn't a difficult call, it wasn't even high stakes—but I was dragging. I had already rearranged my desk, cleared my inbox, looked out the window. My brain was making deals: maybe I'll call after lunch. Maybe I'll do research first. Maybe I'll follow them on Zillow to see if they update their listing. None of it was real work. It was DMN in full swing—storytelling mode, prediction mode, avoidance mode.

I broke the loop by doing one thing: I clicked the contact and typed a single sentence in my call notes. Just that motion flipped the circuit. Then I stood up, walked once around the room, sat back down, and hit dial. The first five seconds were still awkward. The voice on the other end didn't sound welcoming. But I asked my opening question, and after ten seconds, I was no longer dragging—I was in the call. I had switched networks. I was doing.

That one phone call turned into a house listing. Then a sale. Then a thank-you text. Later, a referral. And eventually, a friend. A client for life. Not all calls turn out like that—many lead nowhere. But even one like this? Worth it.

The temptation is to trick yourself with false positivity. To pump yourself up with phrases like "I love this!" or "Let's crush it!" But the truth is, you don't need to lie to yourself to get moving. You don't have to love the task. You just have to do the task. Acknowledging the drag isn't weakness. It's precision.

A quiet acknowledgment like "This isn't exciting—and that's okay," followed by a simple start move, is often more effective than pretending to be hyped. You're not trying to manufacture excitement. You're trying to interrupt inertia. That's what starting does. It breaks the loop.

Some people use a mantra or inner phrase—I call it a True Whisper. Not a slogan, not a chant. Just a short line that grounds you when the drag starts swirling. Something like: "Start is strength." "One contact at a time." "Calm and confident in the face of uncertainty." The point isn't motivation. It's activation.

Think about it. How many times have you dreaded starting a workout, only to feel completely different five minutes in? How many phone calls have you avoided for an hour, only to realize the first one wasn't that bad? The story in your head before the task is rarely accurate. But if you never start, that story becomes reality.

This chapter isn't about stoicism or grit or crushing it through the pain. It's about being honest. The brain resists for a reason—it's conserving energy, avoiding uncertainty. But the moment you make even the smallest physical move, you're rewiring the circuitry. You're teaching your brain what's actually happening now—not what it imagined might happen.

This is the reframe: starting doesn't require a good attitude. It just requires a move.

Let the others chase motivation. You know better. You know that the real switch flips the moment you start—not the moment you feel like it. So next time the drag hits, don't fake it. Don't avoid it. Just name it. Then move anyway.

Chapter 29 — Grit Starts at Zero

Everyone wants to talk about grit like it's a crown they've earned, something they wear like a badge. But real grit doesn't show up when things are smooth. It starts the moment you lose the map, the moment there's no audience, no recognition, no applause. Real grit starts at zero.

Not zero as in a score. Zero as in nothing—no momentum, no energy, no reason to go except that quiet voice that says: go anyway.

You see this in business, in sports, in any field where performance matters. People talk about hustle, post the photos of wins and achievements. But that's not grit. That's what comes after. That's the harvest.

Grit is the morning after the deal falls through and you have no backup. Grit is the day the inbox is empty. Grit is staring at your calendar, knowing nobody's calling. The work feels like a bad engine running on fumes. That's the zero. And what you do in that space isn't magic—it's showing up anyway. Making the calls. Taking the swings. Doing what you can with what you have. That's where the muscle builds. That's where real grit lives.

You see the same thing in sports. A pro golfer practicing the same swing over and over—maybe fifty times. No coach standing by. No crowd. No tournament. Just repetition. Pure boredom. That's the zero. It's the bucket of balls no one sees. The practice round before the flight to the tournament. The five-foot putt that means nothing and everything at the same time. You watch amateurs—they hit one good shot and want praise. But pros? They hit a good shot and go back to the ball. Because they know grit starts where comfort ends.

Researchers have found similar truths. One long-term study of engineering students showed that the highest performers weren't the ones who solved problems fastest—they were the ones who tolerated staying stuck the longest before quitting. They built resilience by enduring the discomfort of zero, and that tolerance later paid off with bigger breakthroughs. Another small study suggested that people who failed early but kept showing up developed more confidence than those who had quick wins. It wasn't about talent. It was about staying in the game when nothing was paying off yet.

Ask any filmmaker, writer, or musician you admire. The real grind wasn't after the deal or the book launch. It was the years before—when nobody was watching, nobody cared, and every attempt fell flat. There's a quiet misery to making things in obscurity. No metrics. No deadline. No praise. Just discipline. One writer said he wrote for six years before a single essay got published. He said the hardest part wasn't the rejections. It was the mornings he had to convince himself that the act of writing itself was worth it—even if no one ever saw it. That's grit starting at zero.

People want to start when it feels good—when they have a new system, a fresh plan, a sunny day. But that's not grit. Grit shows up when energy is low, motivation is gone, and no one is watching. Grit is what you do when the dopamine's gone and the only reward is that you did it anyway. You want to know how to outperform the ones with more tools, more time, more help? You go when you have nothing. You start when the odds are low. You create momentum from a standstill. That's how you build an edge no one can fake. Because grit built at zero doesn't collapse under pressure—it grows stronger.

I once heard someone say, "I don't chase business—I wait for it to come to me." And I thought: what happens when it doesn't? That's not grit. That's comfort. Grit is the guy who shows up every day to the gym at 6 a.m., whether he slept well or not. Or the writer who puts down 500 words even when they hate everything they're writing. Or the founder who ships the update after midnight with no users yet. Momentum isn't something you ride. It's something you create. And it always starts from zero.

Most people wait for a spark—some inspiration or sign that it's the right time. But the pros strike the match themselves. One call. One swing. One sentence. That's how you beat inertia. Not by waiting to feel good, but by moving anyway.

If you're at zero right now, good. That's your edge. Most people never act unless they feel ready—which means most people never act at all. But you're still here. You already know.

Grit doesn't start when you're winning. It starts when you've got nothing. No momentum. No rhythm. No reason. Just one small move—and the guts to keep making it. That's grit. And it always starts at zero.

Chapter 30 — Building a Streak, One Day at a Time

Momentum doesn't come in waves. It comes in reps. It doesn't arrive fully formed like a spark from the sky. It's something you stack—one day, then another, then another. The most powerful mental pattern you can build isn't intensity; it's consistency. The ability to show up—not just once with force, but again and again with discipline—is what creates real momentum.

We tend to think in sprints. "I'll go hard this week." "I'll knock everything out in one big push." Maybe it works for a day or two, but then life interrupts. You skip a day. Then two. And suddenly the effort collapses. That's why streaks matter. Streaks give you something stronger than motivation—they give you identity.

You're not someone hoping to write. You're someone who's written five days in a row. You're not trying to get in shape. You've worked out for thirteen straight days. You're not guessing if you can sell. You've made thirty calls a day for eighteen days. Every streak is a private ledger, proof that your behavior matches your intention. And when your brain sees evidence, it stops resisting. It starts cooperating.

A 2013 study published in *Psychological Science* tracked habit formation across different daily routines. The researchers found that consecutive action—even in small doses—shifted how participants saw themselves. A task done enough days in a row stopped being a task and started being part of identity. There was no magic number of days. What mattered was that the actions were consecutive.

That's why streaks matter more than goals. A goal is an outcome. A streak is a system.

Jerry Seinfeld once explained his writing habit as "don't break the chain." Every day he wrote, he marked a big red X on his calendar. The win wasn't writing a great joke. The win was keeping the chain intact. Over time, the chain itself became motivation. The streak turned into a form of identity protection.

This works because of loss aversion. Behavioral science shows that people hate losing progress more than they enjoy gaining it. Once a streak is built, your brain will fight to preserve it—even when you're tired, busy, or unmotivated. The chain is proof of investment, and the mind protects what it has invested in.

But here's the key: the streak doesn't have to be intense. It just has to be intact. If the bar is too high, resistance will beat you. That's where "minimum viable streaks" come in. Can't run five miles? Jog for ten minutes. Can't write a chapter? Write a paragraph. Can't make twenty calls? Make three. The day still counts. The chain is unbroken.

One musician in New York has done this for over a decade. Every morning before 9 a.m., he records one short improvisation at the piano and saves it to a private folder. No audience. No applause. No pressure. Just one recording a day. The practice has given him a calm clarity in live performance that can't be faked. Not because he was inspired every morning, but because he refused to break the chain.

Your streak doesn't need a grand launch; it needs a start. Pick one daily action, set the bar low enough that you can't not do it, track it, protect it, and don't break the chain, because streaks build identity, identity builds resilience, and resilience builds outcomes. Start small, go daily, protect the chain—that's how momentum is built, one unbroken day at a time.

Chapter 31 — Fire Doesn't Burn Without Oxygen

Everyone loves fire. We glorify it—ambition, drive, hustle, intensity. Entire industries are built around stoking it. Motivation videos, performance coaches, personal development routines—it's all about adding fuel. The logic seems sound: if you're not getting the results you want, you probably need to go harder. Wake up earlier. Grind longer. Eliminate excuses.

But that's only half the story. Fire doesn't burn from fuel alone. It burns because there's oxygen. Take away the oxygen and it dies, no matter how much fuel you throw on it. The flame chokes, sputters, and vanishes. And that's exactly what happens to people who live in constant noise, clutter, urgency, or emotional chaos. They don't burn out because they lack drive. They burn out because they can't breathe.

You don't need more fuel—you need space. Structure. Breathing room. Focus. Without it, your best ideas suffocate before they take root. Your productive hours get buried under low-value tasks. Judgment clouds, instincts dull, and clarity slips away. You're still moving, still working, but beneath the surface the fire is dying.

I learned this lesson the hard way. Early on, I prided myself on outworking everyone. My calendar was packed. Days bled into nights. Every call, every email, every meeting—I said yes to all of it. For a while, it worked. Money came in, the name got known, momentum built. But eventually the sharpness dulled. I forgot things. I double-booked. I was reactive instead of intentional. It wasn't fuel I was missing. It was oxygen.

That's when I started treating oxygen as a resource. I carved out uninterruptible blocks in my schedule. I left margins between appointments. I took walks without my phone. I said no more often. And something shifted. My focus sharpened, my decisions improved, and my output actually went up—not because I worked harder, but because I could finally breathe.

This is the part almost nobody talks about. Everyone's obsessed with adding more—more tools, more systems, more productivity hacks. The pros learn to subtract. They cut the noise that doesn't move the needle. They protect their inputs. Not because they're rigid, but because they understand attention is finite. Waste it, and you smother your own fire.

That's why elite athletes build recovery into their training. The muscle doesn't grow in the gym—it grows in the space between workouts. The best minds in business do the same. Warren Buffett reads for hours. Jeff Bezos cleared his mornings for big decisions. Cal Newport calls it time blocking: putting the important work on the calendar and defending it like your life depends on it. Different methods, same principle: protect the oxygen.

Most people don't. They fill every gap with meetings, pings, scrolling, and shallow work. And then they wonder why they feel busy but make no progress. Burnout isn't from doing too much. It's from doing too much of the wrong things with no room to recover.

I once coached a young agent who was stuck in that trap. She worked twelve-hour days, stacked calls on calls, made content, trained her team—but nothing was landing. Her leads weren't converting and her energy was scattered. I looked at her schedule and asked: "Where's your thinking time?" There wasn't any.

We stripped her calendar down. Cut the fake productivity. Built in blank space. Within sixty days, she was sharper, her messaging tightened, and her conversion rate tripled. Nothing new was added. We just let her breathe.

That's the leverage oxygen gives you. Better decisions. Faster recovery. Long-term sustainability. You stop drowning in noise and start building with intention.

Ask yourself: What's burning fuel in your life but giving back no oxygen? Maybe it's constant email checking. Maybe it's endless comparison online. Maybe it's busywork that looks important but isn't. Find the leak and shut it.

This isn't about slowing down or being soft; it's about control. You can go fast, but not at the cost of clarity, because without oxygen the fire collapses, and with oxygen it becomes something more than a flash in the pan—it becomes a furnace. Fire is what people see, but oxygen is what makes it possible, and that's what you protect.

Chapter 32 — Start Signals: Breaking the Autopilot Loop

Most of life runs on autopilot—routines, reactions, default settings. Some of that works beautifully in your favor. Autopilot is the reason you can brush your teeth without thinking, make coffee half-asleep, or drive a familiar route and barely remember the turns. In the gym, autopilot carries you from push-up five to push-up fifty because your body already knows the rhythm. But autopilot has blind spots. It disappears at two critical moments: the first rep and the final rep. You don't get the benefit of automated momentum until you've begun, and it abandons you when fatigue hits and finishing requires intention instead of habit. Those two edges—starting and finishing—are where most people stall.

This is why hesitation feels heavier than the work itself. The loop that keeps you stuck isn't laziness; it's the brain's default script whispering the same old lines: It's not the right time. I'm too tired. I don't have a plan. I'll start tomorrow. These loops pretend to be logic, but they're just patterned avoidance. They keep you in place while convincing you that stillness is safety.

People love to blame their hesitation on caveman mythology—as if their brain is hardwired to freeze at every shadow. But the research is clear: habits are built from repetition, not prehistoric danger. Modern neuroscience has mapped habit formation far better than evolutionary storytelling ever could. The loops that hold you back today weren't shaped by mammoths; they were shaped by yesterday's choices, last month's procrastination, and the grooves carved by years of repetition. You built the loop. And that means you can break it.

Breaking it doesn't require force or inspiration. It requires what I call a Start Signal—a short, personal cue that snaps you out of autopilot at the exact moment it's trying to keep you stuck. A Start Signal is not a mantra, not a motivational speech, and not some performance hack. It's a simple phrase that interrupts the automatic pattern long enough for you to do the smallest possible version of the task. Something like: This one step matters. Start now, fix later. Five minutes is enough. I've done harder things. These aren't affirmations. They are disruptors. Their only job is to tilt you toward movement.

The science behind this is straightforward. When you hesitate, your brain activates the Default Mode Network—the DMN— the part responsible for rumination, daydreaming, and internal chatter. It loops the same thoughts, magnifying doubts and predictions, making the task seem larger than it is. But the moment you begin—even with the smallest physical action— your brain switches to the Task-Positive Network, or TPN. This system is built for execution. It handles focus, motor control, and problem solving. And the critical point: the two systems cannot run simultaneously. If the DMN is in charge, you stall. If the TPN is in charge, you move. The Start Signal is the lever that flips the switch.

That flip doesn't have to be heroic. It just has to be real. Think of the last pushup in a set. Autopilot can carry you through the middle reps, but the first rep and the last five require conscious engagement. They require a signal—not motivation, but intention. Without that micro-signal, you stay frozen at rep zero forever. And the same thing happens with calls, writing, workouts, paperwork, and every other meaningful task in your life.

And this applies beyond work. A single Start Signal can change your relationships. One quick "hello" with a smile has started more meaningful relationships than just about anything else. It's the smallest possible action, but it flips the network. You move from rumination to connection. From looping thoughts to lived experience. The entire trajectory of a friendship—or something more—can begin with that one tiny cue.

The mistake people make is attacking their entire operating system instead of addressing the exact point where hesitation shows up. You don't need to reinvent your life. You don't need a new personality, a new planner, or a whole new identity. You need a cue that meets you right at the friction point. A Start Signal cuts through the fog at the precise moment inertia tries to win.

You already use Start Signals without realizing it. Runners tie their shoes. Writers open the document. Agents place the notepad on the desk. These aren't tasks—they're gateways. Physical cues that activate the TPN and disable the DMN long enough to push you into motion. When you combine that physical cue with a verbal one, you create a habit interrupter that is almost impossible for the brain to ignore.

And there is a place for autopilot. You want it during the middle reps, the sustained sessions, the repetitive parts of your craft. You want autopilot when you're already in the flow. That's what allows the writer to draft pages without stopping, the athlete to stay in rhythm, the agent to make twenty calls in a row without thinking. Autopilot is a gift once you're moving. But it is useless before the first step and unreliable at the finish line. That's where the Start Signal earns its keep.

I've seen Start Signals rescue careers. I coached an agent years ago who had the skills, the charm, the market knowledge—but she could never start her day. She'd sit at her desk in a fog, scrolling, organizing, delaying. We created one line for her: Start with one call. That was it. No pressure, no scoreboard. She wrote it on a sticky note and put it on her monitor. Every morning, the moment hesitation hit, she said it quietly. That one call created two. Those two created momentum. Within six months, she was one of the top performers in her office. Not because she changed who she was, but because she interrupted who she wasn't.

Autopilot will never kick in at the beginning. It can't. The brain has no script until you create one. That's why the first five minutes of anything feel heavier than the next fifty. They're the only minutes that require a decision. After that, you're riding the system you built.

Your job is to master the ignition point. To recognize exactly when the loop starts whispering and cut through it with a signal strong enough to override the pattern. This isn't mysticism. It's a skill—a tool you can use anywhere hesitation appears.

Start Signals don't eliminate fear. They don't erase resistance. They just give you a crack in the old loop—wide enough for action to slip through. And once action enters, everything changes. DMN quiets. TPN takes over. You move. And once you're moving, momentum handles the rest.

Build your signal. Make it short. Make it yours. Use it exactly when the loop tightens. That is how you break autopilot. That is how you start again—not with certainty, but with interruption, clarity, and one decisive move in the right direction.

Chapter 33 — The Habit Loop and How to Interrupt It

There's a pattern behind every action you repeat—good or bad. Most people live inside these loops without realizing it. The habit loop is simple, powerful, and if you don't interrupt it, it will run your life.

Every loop has three parts: cue, routine, reward. A cue triggers you—time of day, emotion, place. The routine is the behavior. Smoke the cigarette. Scroll the feed. Skip the workout. The reward is the hit—dopamine, relief, stimulation. Repeat this long enough and you're no longer choosing. You're obeying.

Habits don't just shape behavior. They shape identity. Eat junk food enough times and you don't just eat poorly—you become the person who can't resist. Check your phone enough and you become the one who's always distracted. Your life is not the sum of your goals. It's the sum of your loops.

One of mine showed up at 4:30 p.m. almost every day. Foggy brain, low energy. Without thinking, I'd grab a snack. It wasn't hunger—it was a loop. Cue: fatigue. Routine: eat. Reward: a quick sugar bump. Once I saw the pattern, I added friction. No food after four unless I walked outside first. That five-minute walk reset the loop, and half the time the craving vanished. It wasn't discipline. It was disruption.

This is the key. You don't break loops by blaming yourself. You break them by spotting the script. Once you see it, you can change it.

Science backs this up. In a classic MIT study, rats ran a maze. At first their brains lit up with activity—they were searching for the path. But after enough repetitions, the middle of the maze went dark. Only the start and the end fired. That's a habit loop. Cue → routine → reward. The brain stopped thinking. It just ran code.

The same thing happens to us. Scroll Instagram, snack late, avoid hard work—it isn't a fresh decision each time. It's an automated shortcut firing. But awareness changes everything. At UCLA, researchers found that labeling an urge—literally saying, "I feel anxious and want to snack"—reduced activity in the craving centers of the brain. Naming it is like hitting a circuit breaker. You buy yourself time and control.

So how do you interrupt the loop? Start small. Choose one habit. Track the cue. Is it time, place, or emotion? Then map the routine—exactly what you do when the cue hits. Next, identify the real reward. Are you hungry, or bored? Tired, or avoiding something? Once you see it clearly, insert friction. Ten push-ups before the snack. Airplane mode before bed. A short walk before opening email. The goal isn't perfection—it's disruption.

Your environment is part of the loop too. Rearrange it. Clean the desk. Move the phone charger out of the bedroom. Hide the triggers. Small changes create breaks in the code and give you breathing room to choose something different.

Then comes the identity shift. Don't say, "I'm trying to stop." Say, "I'm not someone who does that anymore." Behavior rewrites belief. The language you use becomes the evidence your brain accepts, and repetition cements it.

And don't fear failure. A study from a pharmaceutical company running smoking-cessation programs found that the more times people tried to quit, the more likely they eventually succeeded. Each failed attempt wasn't wasted—it trained them. Persistence wasn't a weakness. It was predictive.

So if you've tried to stop ten times and slipped back, good— that means you're closer than the person who hasn't tried at all, because every attempt weakens the old loop and strengthens the new. You're not your cravings, not your procrastination, not the tired version of yourself at 4:30; you're just running a script, and you can rewrite it, one loop at a time, one start at a time—that's how you take control.

Chapter 34 — Crafting Personal Start Signals for Focus

Every day your mind is pulled in a dozen directions. Notifications, headlines, worries, comparison, distraction — all of it competes for attention. Most people try to fight this chaos by piling on more tools, more hacks, more lists. They respond to noise with more noise. But clarity doesn't come from complexity. It comes from a simple internal anchor: a Start Signal.

A Start Signal is not a slogan or a motivational quote you tape to your mirror. It isn't meant to inspire you or pump you up. It is a private cue that cuts through hesitation in the exact moment you begin to drift. It's a phrase short enough to remember, personal enough to matter, and honest enough to reset you when discipline starts slipping. The best Start Signals don't try to create emotion. They create direction.

Every performer, builder, athlete, or creator who operates at a high level relies on something like this. They might not call it a Start Signal, but it functions the same way. When distraction creeps in, when pressure rises, when the drift begins, a single line snaps them back into presence. It recalibrates them. It reminds their mind what the body is here to do. It doesn't create motivation — it restores focus.

I needed mine during a season when I was working hard but not deeply. I was reacting to everything, chasing inbox pings, and mistaking movement for progress. Nothing was sticking. Nothing felt sharp. My Start Signal became: *"Nothing matters but the work."* It wasn't poetic, but it did the job. The moment the noise started creeping in, that line cut through it. It didn't make me feel good. It made me get back to work.

Some Start Signals come from defiance — words spoken after being underestimated. Others come from memory — promises made to people who aren't here anymore. Others come from vision — the person you're trying to become. The origin doesn't matter. What matters is that the phrase is real to you. A Start Signal should feel like truth, not hype.

Felix Baumgartner, the skydiver who jumped from 128,000 feet in 2012, literally carried his Start Signal on his arm. Tattooed on his skin: *Born to Fly*. He explained that the words weren't motivation. They were identity. They reminded him of who he believed he was when doubt crept in. That belief carried him through one of the most dangerous human feats ever attempted.

Muhammad Ali had his own signal. "Float like a butterfly, sting like a bee" wasn't just a catchphrase for the crowd. It was a tactical instruction wrapped in rhythm — a reminder of how he fought and who he was in the ring. It kept him grounded in strategy when chaos broke out around him. These lines weren't for show. They were internal anchors disguised as poetry.

Crafting your Start Signal isn't complicated, but it *does* require honesty. Begin by looking at the moments you consistently lose focus. Where does the drift happen? Is it the first five minutes of a task? The point where frustration appears? Late afternoon when your energy dips? Your signal belongs in the exact place where you tend to slip.

Then look at the opposite side of that struggle. What becomes possible when you stay in motion instead of drifting? What outcome actually matters to you? What version of you shows up when you're locked in and sharp? Your Start Signal should be a direct line to that version. Short, raw, unpolished — something like: "Earn it." "Start clean." "Don't break the chain." "You're not done yet." "Back to work."

This is how you beat the drift. If you don't feed your brain a deliberate signal, the world fills the space with its own signals — distraction, comparison, urgency, fear. People who drift aren't weak. They're silent. They don't give their mind a command, so the mind defaults to autopilot. People who stay focused carry a line that keeps them anchored.

Write your Start Signal and refine it until it feels true. A Start Signal is the bridge between intention and action, and once you learn to use it, the noise loses its power.

Chapter 35 — Implementing Start Signals in Daily Life

So now you've got the Start Signal. Maybe it's just a few words. Maybe it hit you like a steel dart. Maybe it took a few tries to get the right one. Doesn't matter. What matters is what you do next. Most people stop here. They have the phrase, write it down, feel good for a day or two, and then the storm rolls back in. They drift, default, and assume the Start Signal "didn't work." That's not failure—it's friction. And friction is exactly where the signal belongs.

A Start Signal is a precision tool, embedded in your day like a code override. Old software is already running—loops you built years ago. You don't erase that with one insight. You override it through repetition, environment, and deliberate reinforcement.

First rule: externalize it. If your Start Signal only lives in your head, it won't survive. Write it where you'll see it—on a sticky note, your lock screen, your notebook. Not as decoration, but as deployment. These reminders aren't about positivity; they're operational markers telling your brain where the new program begins.

Second: map the battlefield. Track when you stall or drift. Is it the alarm clock? The midday crash? The quiet hours after dinner? Don't guess—pinpoint. The signal is useless if you don't know where to use it. The moment of failure is usually predictable, and once you see the pattern, you know exactly where the signal needs to intercept the loop.

Now install it. If mornings are chaos, and your Start Signal is

"First brick," tie it to action: set an 8 a.m. alarm labeled with the phrase, and don't touch coffee until you've moved one thing forward. Cue, routine, reward. The loop rewired. People wait for the signal to create the behavior, but it's the behavior—linked tightly to the signal—that locks the system in place.

Angela, a cardiac nurse, carried a long-stalled dream of becoming a photographer. The loop in her head said, "You're too tired. You're not an artist." Her father used to tell her on hikes, "Beauty doesn't beg—you go get it." She wrote that down: "Go get it." It became her Start Signal. She kept her camera bag in the car, pulled over on her commute when the light was good, and started shooting. Five minutes here, ten there. It built a rhythm. That signal didn't just win her a photo contest—it gave her a new operating system.

Science backs this up. A Stanford study on "implementation intentions" showed that people who mapped out when, where, and how they would act were two to three times more likely to follow through. It wasn't motivation that mattered—it was specificity. The signal worked because it had a plan. It sat at the intersection of intention and execution, reducing the friction that usually kills momentum.

So give yours a plan. Tie it to the loop you want to interrupt. Make hesitation more painful than action. If your Start Signal is "One page before bed," put your journal on the pillow. If it's "Five breaths before email," tape it to your monitor. If it's "Show up before I'm ready," schedule something public that forces the move. The world responds to what you commit to in structure, not what you daydream about in private.

Your life already runs on whispers—old ones. You've been repeating them for years: "I'm not a morning person." "I can't follow through." "It's not my season." They loop quietly until they feel like truth. That's why you need to replace them—not with hype, but with something truer, sharper, and tied to an action that contradicts the old script.

One last ritual makes it stick. At the end of the day, ask yourself, "Where did I use my Start Signal today?" Find the moment. Then say, "Good. Again tomorrow." That's reinforcement. That's identity building. You're not rewarding the outcome. You're reinforcing the pattern of showing up, which is the only pattern that ever matters.

And don't expect one Start Signal to last forever. They evolve as you do. The line that gets you moving today might not fit six months from now. That's progress, not failure. Upgrade it when the mission changes. Your operating system should grow with you.

You don't need shelves of mantras. You need one line at a time—sharp enough to cut through the noise, tied to action, repeated until it becomes your new baseline. That's how you break the old code. That's how you rewire. And that's how you start—again and again—on purpose.

Chapter 36 — The Science Behind Start Signaling

By now, you've heard this idea more than once. Not because I like to repeat myself, but because if you lock this in, everything else in your life gets easier. That's not hype—it's wiring. Business, body, mornings, mindset—all of it shifts when you master the art of interrupting yourself and starting on command.

That's why this chapter isn't in the beginning. It's here as payoff—for the reader who kept going, who didn't skim, who's been wrestling with the noise. If that's you, here's the truth: this isn't motivational theory. It's science. And once you see the mechanics, the signals hit harder, and the results come faster.

Start Signaling works because it taps into how the brain actually functions. You're not pumping yourself up. You're giving your system a cue. And the reason it works isn't fluff—it's leverage.

The brain craves clarity. It thrives on simplicity. Feed it a phrase that's short, sharp, and emotionally anchored, and it pays attention. That's what a Start Signal is: a clean, compact cue that slips past resistance and flips the ignition switch.

Why does it work? Because the brain is built for speed, not complexity. In high-stress moments, the prefrontal cortex—the rational decision-maker—gets overloaded. More options mean more paralysis. But short, emotionally charged words activate the salience network, the part of the brain that flags what matters and drives action.

This ties to a principle called cognitive fluency: the easier something is to process, the more true and actionable it feels. That's why slogans stick. That's why mantras endure. That's why your Start Signal—if it's short and repeated—doesn't just sound good. It sticks.

And repetition matters. Behavioral scientists like B.J. Fogg and Charles Duhigg showed how habit loops run: cue → routine → reward. Most people fail not because they lack desire, but because they lack a cue. A Start Signal is that cue. It's the trigger that flips you into motion, which leads to a reward—even if it's just the relief of starting. Over time, the loop strengthens.

Dopamine deepens the effect. It's not just the "pleasure chemical." It's the motivation chemical. Studies show dopamine spikes not only when we get a reward, but when we expect one. Condition your brain to expect movement after a Start Signal, and it becomes a self-fulfilling cycle. The signal fires, dopamine flows, action follows.

In a world of noise, that's defense as much as offense. We switch tasks every 40 seconds on average. Attention isn't just scarce—it's under siege. A Start Signal works because it doesn't require silence or perfect conditions. It just has to be repeated until your brain recognizes it like a lighthouse in a storm.

This overlaps with implementation intentions—the if-then wiring studied by Peter Gollwitzer at NYU. People who pre-decide their response to obstacles ("If I feel resistance, then I use this signal…") are dramatically more likely to act. A Start Signal becomes that preloaded plan. Over time, the gap between impulse and action shrinks. That's not discipline. That's circuitry.

Layer in self-efficacy—the belief that you can actually do the thing. Albert Bandura called it the top predictor of behavior change. Every time you signal yourself and move, you reinforce: I don't stall, I start. That micro-proof compounds until it becomes identity.

And don't overlook pattern interruption. Loops run because they're automatic—scrolling, snacking, delaying. A Start Signal like "Do it tired" breaks the trance. The brain responds to novelty, especially when it's a command. That's why even small phrases work. They're jolts of signal in a world of static.

Think of a track race. The runners are ready, tense, waiting. Does the race start with a speech? A checklist? A debate? No. It starts with one sound: the gunshot. Pure signal. No explanation. Just go. That's what a Start Signal is. Your personal starter pistol.

And here's the deeper magic: when you repeat a phrase during action, the brain tags it with emotion. Say it while moving, and later that signal recalls the whole win. It stops being words. It becomes anchored experience.

So don't over complicate it. Don't chase clever lines. Just make it short, real, and yours. Repeat it until your system obeys without question. That's when it stops being a trick and becomes your ignition.

The science ends there. The devotion begins after. Because once you've got your Start Signal, analysis is done. The only thing left is the repeat.

Chapter 37 — Fall in Love With the Start. Repeat.

The world worships the finish line. Champagne at the ribbon. The big reveal. "Congratulations, you did it!" That dopamine spike at the end—people chase it their whole lives. The raise, the close, the trophy, the weight loss photo. Everything is built to make us crave that moment. But what if that's not where the real power is? What if the people who win, again and again, aren't the ones who idolize the finish—but the ones who know how to fall in love with the start?

If you can learn to love the beginning—the blank canvas, the unopened door, the untouched keyboard, the first rep, the first sentence, the first brick—if that's what gives you the high, then finishing becomes a byproduct. You'll keep starting, and you'll keep winning, because you're addicted to ignition, not outcome.

Back in school, most kids dreaded the start of an exam. They'd stall, flip through pages, fiddle with pencils, peek at the clock. Not me. If I was prepared, I loved it. Loved the feel of writing my name at the top. That was the moment I knew I was in control. That I was about to attack the thing, not survive it. The starting line wasn't scary—it was a declaration. That tells you something.

We're conditioned from childhood to think about the end. Finish your vegetables. Finish your homework. Finish your chores. Get to the weekend. Graduate. Achieve. Everything is driven by delayed gratification, and that's fine—until it trains you to hate the beginning. Until it wires you to see the start as a necessary evil, a roadblock before the reward. So you delay it.

THE MAGIC OF STARTING

Avoid it. Make excuses. You wait until you're "ready." And
then you wonder why nothing ever builds.

Here's the truth: the people who build unstoppable momentum
aren't obsessed with finishing—they're in love with beginning.
And they do it over and over and over again. Falling in love
with the start isn't about denying the value of completion. It's
about understanding that nothing gets finished unless it gets
started. And more importantly—nothing meaningful gets
repeated unless starting becomes a way of life.

So how do you do that? How do you train yourself to love the
ignition point when every part of you is wired to resist it? Start
by finding your Main Start Signal.

If you've made it this far in the book, you already know what a
Start Signal is: a short phrase that cuts through the mental
static, resets your system, and sparks motion. But there's
something deeper than having a few signals that work. There's
the Main Start Signal—the one you build your day around. The
one that aligns with your soul like a tuning fork.

It's personal. No one else needs to understand it. It doesn't
have to make sense to the world. It only needs to activate you.
Some people already have theirs—they just haven't recognized
it. Others need to find it. But you'll know it when it lands. It
hits like a line from a movie that somehow feels written for
you. It's the one phrase you return to when life feels heavy or
scattered or flat. It might be something primal like "One brick."
Or spiritual like "Move in faith." Maybe it's "Carry it forward,"
or "Just one more."

These aren't motivational slogans—they're identity anchors.

When it's yours, you don't need to shout it. You just think it, and you move. Your Main Start Signal is your ignition code. It bypasses hesitation. It builds a bridge back to action. One signal, repeated, becomes a rhythm. And once you've got rhythm, you're dangerous.

This is not just poetic. Science backs it up. In 2018, researchers at the University of Zurich published a study in Motivation and Emotion showing that anticipating the start of a meaningful task triggered more consistent motivation than anticipating the finish. We've been told only the end gives us the dopamine hit, but their data showed the opposite: people who learned to focus on beginnings developed stronger follow-through. The start itself created a reward loop—if you trained your brain to value it.

Another angle: anticipatory dopamine. Most people think dopamine appears only at the payoff. Not true. The strongest spike comes right before you begin. The brain is already warming up your chemistry for action. But if you stall, you never cash it in. Learning to move at that anticipatory peak locks you into a cycle where the start becomes the high.

Now look at history. Thomas Edison wasn't addicted to the final lightbulb—he was addicted to beginning the next attempt. Each failure wasn't a failure to him; it was ignition. Another start. Another run at the puzzle. He loved the spark more than the finished product. Same with the Wright brothers. They didn't wait for the perfect blueprint. They built, tested, crashed, rebuilt. They fell in love with starting over. Progress belongs to the people who never get bored of beginning again.

Children understand this instinctively. Watch a kid on a swing.

They don't say, "That was fun, now I'm done." They say, "Again, again, again!" The first push is sacred every time. G.K. Chesterton wrote that perhaps God Himself tells the sun each morning, "Do it again." The idea is simple: maybe repetition isn't dull—maybe it's divine.

Adults, on the other hand, treat repetition like a burden. Same tasks. Same mornings. Same calls. They see every start as punishment. I once knew an agent who'd answer "Same old shit" anytime someone asked how he was doing. Eventually he burned out, bitter and broke. That's what happens when every start feels like a penalty. You want the edge? Fall in love with the start.

So how do you retrain yourself? First, build rituals that protect the ignition point. Make the first move sacred. Write your Main Start Signal on a sticky note and put it on your keyboard. Create a "first five minutes" rule—no phone, no email, no drifting. Just one real move toward your mission.

Pair the start with something pleasurable. First brick, then coffee. First sentence, then breakfast. You're not chasing the whole workout or the whole chapter. You're chasing ignition. Next, lower the bar. Don't demand perfect starts. Demand starts, period. If your rule is "run one mile every day," you'll flinch. If your rule is "step outside in running shoes," you'll move. And once you move, the body follows. The brain hates stopping once it's started.

Finally, repeat without apology. Don't wait for novelty. Don't stall for inspiration. The start is the inspiration. Condition yourself to crave the first rep, the first stroke, the first page. Over time, the start becomes the high.

That's why "the mindset of starting" beats "the mindset of learning." Growth mindset is great, but it's passive. It believes in potential. Starting mindset is active. It expresses potential. It's the ignition between theory and transformation. Momentum doesn't appear out of nowhere. You spark it. You create it by starting small and repeating. Again and again until it's second nature.

Fall in love with the start. Repeat. That's the mantra. If you only remember one thing from this book, let it be this—not the finish line, not the applause, not the reveal. Just this: Start. Repeat. Start again.

Write it down. Tape it to your dashboard. Engrave it in your routines. This is your weapon. The world will throw chaos, distraction, noise, and pressure. Let it. You've mastered the ignition point. And once you own the start, you own the day. And once you own the day, you own your life.

Chapter 38 — The Starting Point

Vince Lombardi once walked into a locker room after his team had been humiliated. These were professionals—talented, disciplined, hardened. They sat in silence, waiting for a speech or a plan. Lombardi gave none of it. He held up a football and said, "Gentlemen, this is a football." It sounds simple—maybe even patronizing. But that was the point. He was resetting the system. When everything falls apart, when noise creeps in, complexity suffocates clarity. You don't rebuild from theory. You rebuild from the thing itself.

You start again. Not with a speech. Not with planning. With the object. The ball. The instrument. The thing in hand that calls you back. That's the starting point.

Objects carry memory. They anchor motion. The grip, the texture, the weight—they whisper motion to your body before your brain can talk you out of it. The tennis racket, the notebook, the camera—they're not props. They're doorways back into the loop of doing.

I feel it every time I cradle a trout in cold water. The flash of its color, the life in its gills—they ground me. That moment isn't about catch or success. It's about contact. It's a reminder. That's my starting point.

Phil Mickelson knows this. Before he ever swings, he walks the course. He reads the grain of the grass, the texture of the fringe. His ritual isn't about the shot. It's about returning to the ground. Jerry Rice knew it too. He arrived early on game day, walking the turf, feeling the seams underfoot, imagining where he'd cut and explode. His object was the field itself—the terrain that framed his motion. Not hype. Not talk. That contact grounded him to the game.

And it's not just athletes or anglers. Stanislavski taught actors that props were more than decoration—they were portals. A hat. A letter. A piece of furniture. The object becomes a vessel for identity. You don't summon the part. You touch the thing, and the part wakes.

This is the starting point. Motivation doesn't precede motion. Motion precedes motivation. When you touch the object, mirror circuits, procedural memory, sensorimotor systems light up. You don't persuade yourself. You remember.

There's a body of research known as embodied cognition which argues just that: cognition isn't detached from the body. Our minds extend into tools, objects, environments. When you touch a tool you know, neural circuits associated with motion and memory activate as though the tool is part of you. The boundary between hand and object blurs.

In one strand of this science, researchers examine tool-use and how tools become integrated into our sensorimotor systems. When people use a tool repeatedly, their brain begins to treat it like part of their body's extension. After some time, using the tool doesn't feel like "using" it at all—it feels like an extension of your hand. That shift is what allows movement to feel natural again. This is why the object is your reset switch—not metaphor, but mechanism.

Now find your version of "the football." It doesn't need to be grand—a pen, a brush, a camera, a journal, a tool, a space—just something you don't need to prove anything with, something that invites you to begin. Pick it up, feel it, bring your body, because you already know what comes next once you do.

Chapter 39 — The Start Cell: Time, Action, Start Signal

When life gets too big, shrink it. That's the Start Cell. This chapter isn't about big plans or five-year goals. It's about what you do in the next ten minutes—the next five even. It's about building one container of forward motion and making it repeatable. A Start Cell is the smallest unit of momentum that still moves the needle. It's not theoretical or strategic. It's what you actually do.

We call it a Start Cell for a reason. In biology, a cell is the smallest unit of life. It carries the code, multiplies, and builds everything larger. That's what a Start Cell is for action—the smallest unit of momentum that can expand into more. The word "cell" shows up in other places too—military units, underground groups, even intelligence operations—because a cell is self-contained, powerful, and doesn't need outside permission to act. Whether in biology or strategy, a cell is where growth begins. And in your life, a Start Cell is where momentum begins.

A Start Cell has three parts: time, action, and a Start Signal. That's it. You don't need apps, a perfect schedule, or even energy. You just need to drop into your Start Cell and hit go.

Start with time. Not hours or deep work sessions—just time you can guarantee. Five to fifteen minutes is enough. This is sacred time, not spare time. You carve it out, show up, and run the play. The power of the Start Cell isn't in its length but in its clarity.

Then comes action. Not a task or a to-do item—an action. Something physical, visible, unambiguous. Not thinking about starting or planning to start—actual movement. Type one sentence. Open the editor. Press record. Put your shoes on and walk outside. Send the email. One rep, not one result.

Finally, the trigger: your Start Signal. This is the phrase that drops you into the zone. By now you've probably found your Main Signal—the one that cuts through noise and calls your system to attention. The signal isn't meant for reflection; it's meant for entry. It drops you into your Start Cell on demand. When Sam whispered "One page," his body moved before his doubt could respond.

That's the contract. And that's where the shift begins. Because now you're not wrestling with whether you feel like doing the thing. You're not arguing with yourself. You're running the cell. The Start Cell creates movement, movement creates clarity, clarity creates belief, and belief drives repetition. Suddenly you're not talking about building something—you're building it.

Here's a real example. Sam was a freelance web designer who lost his anchor client—a boutique hotel chain that made up nearly half his income. When they pulled back on marketing during a slow season, the floor fell out from under him. His first thought was, I'm done. His second thought was, I should probably get a job.

For weeks, he sat at his desk, opening Photoshop, scrolling templates, checking freelance job boards. Nothing stuck. The fear was constant: What if that was my last good client? What if I'm just not cut out for this? He even started reworking his résumé for corporate jobs he didn't want.

Finally, he made one small rule: spend ten minutes each morning rebuilding just one page of his portfolio site. Not a full project, not a polished case study—just one page. The first week looked clumsy, half-finished. The second week it had edges. By the third, he had relaunched the whole portfolio. It didn't feel like a breakthrough. It felt like showing up, one Start Cell at a time. But the portfolio was visible again.

One afternoon, a local restaurant group emailed him—they'd found his updated site while searching for a designer to redo their menus and booking platform. That one job turned into three restaurants, then into a referral from their accountant to another client. Within four months, Sam wasn't just back on his feet—he was making more than before. Sam didn't know the term for it, but that was a Start Cell. Time-bound, physical, repeatable. A single container of motion that rebuilt his confidence and his business.

Science backs this up. Researchers at Harvard and University College London have studied what they call "micro-goals"— short, achievable tasks linked to immediate action. Their data shows that breaking large goals into tiny, repeatable units increases dopamine regulation and follow-through by over 60 percent. The brain isn't wired to thrive on grand visions; it's wired to chase the next immediate, clear step. That's exactly what a Start Cell does: it reduces overwhelm, gives the brain a quick win, and builds a reward loop around starting—not finishing.

Now take it out of business. A jazz pianist had gone completely flat after the pandemic. Clubs had shut down. Gigs were gone. Months of silence built into years of doubt. He started to wonder if his best years were behind him. He'd sit at the piano, play a few scales, then walk away. The music wasn't flowing—it was forced.

So he gave himself a different rule: one new improv every morning before breakfast. No audience. No pressure. Just hit record on his phone, play for ten minutes, and stop. Some days the music was jagged, uneven, even bad. But he kept the cell alive. Every morning: ten minutes, one take, no edits.

After a few months, he noticed something: he didn't dread the piano anymore. He looked forward to it. His hands loosened. His instincts sharpened. Eventually, he shared a few of those morning recordings online. A promoter found him. A small gig turned into a steady weekly set. That steady set turned into an album's worth of material.

Like Sam, he hadn't found inspiration—he'd found ignition. His Start Cell carried him out of the slump and back into motion.

That's the engine. A Start Cell is how you turn chaos into a clean ignition loop, on time, every day. And the real win? It scales. Start Cells are stackable. Once you prove one, you build another. You don't need to redesign your life. You just need a rhythm of small, controlled detonations—daily ignition, layered repetition. That's how people go from stuck to sharp.

Here's what it might look like in a day:
7:15 AM – Health Cell. Time: 10 minutes. Action: go outside and walk one loop. Signal: "One brick."
9:00 AM – Work Cell. Time: 15 minutes. Action: open the pitch deck and edit the first slide. Signal: "Move early."
6:30 PM – Writing Cell. Time: 10 minutes. Action: open the draft and write one honest paragraph. Signal: "Start anyway."

That's a day built on ignition—not finish lines or deadlines. Just clean, sharp starts.

Designing your life isn't about balance. It's about repeatable motion. Start Cells give you that—in the middle of a messy week, in a season of uncertainty, in the fog, in the pressure, in the slump. You show up, hit the signal, and move.

The Start Cell replaces guilt with rhythm. To-do lists trigger guilt—you didn't do enough, you forgot a task, you're falling behind—which creates pressure, resistance, and friction, while a Start Cell is simple, honest, daily ignition. It doesn't take hours or inspiration; it takes entry, and entry is everything, because you don't have to win the day—you just have to enter it: time, action, Start Signal. That's the cell, that's the system, and that's how starting begins itself.

Chapter 40 — Why Starting Skews the Math in Your Favor

Motivation is slippery. People treat it like weather—something that rolls in when the conditions are right. They sit around waiting to feel ready, hoping a gust of energy will hit. But motivation isn't weather. It has a structure. A formula. And once you see it, you stop waiting and start manipulating it.

The most accepted equation for motivation looks like this: Motivation = (Expectancy × Value) / (Impulsiveness × Delay). Expectancy is whether you believe you can succeed. Value is how much the outcome matters to you. Impulsiveness is how easily you're distracted. Delay is how far off the reward feels. Put it together and you can see why people stall. You want the thing, you might even believe you can get it, but the denominator kills you. You're distracted, and the payoff feels too far away. The result is low motivation.

Here's the shortcut no one talks about. You can collapse that denominator instantly by starting. Delay drops to zero the second you move. The reward isn't theoretical anymore—it's being built. The gap between you and progress shrinks, and that shift changes the math in your brain. You feel closer, so you feel motivated. Not the other way around. The math favors motion.

I saw this play out with a grad student named Lila who was stuck on her thesis. She'd been circling the topic for weeks, outlining, second-guessing, looking up references she didn't need. Each day the gap between her and the finish line felt bigger. Then one afternoon, she made a decision: she would just write one messy paragraph. Not perfect, not even structured. Just something on the page. That action collapsed the delay. She wasn't waiting to "one day" write her thesis. She was writing it now. By the end of that hour, she had three pages. By the end of the week, she had a working draft. The math shifted because she killed delay with a start.

Expectancy and value—the top half of the equation—take time to build. Belief in yourself doesn't happen overnight. Neither does a deep sense of purpose. But the denominator is fragile. Delay and impulsiveness wobble with the smallest push. If you attack delay, you can tip the entire equation in your favor without waiting to believe, without waiting for purpose to wash over you.

The neuroscience backs this up. Dopamine isn't released only when you win—it spikes in anticipation of progress. A study from Stanford showed that the moment an action begins, the brain's dopamine circuits light up, not because of the end reward, but because of the shift toward it. Rats pressing a lever didn't just light up when the food pellet dropped. Their brains lit up the second they pushed the lever. Humans work the same way. That means even a Start Signal, followed by a small start, primes the brain with momentum chemistry. You don't need to finish to feel the charge. You need to begin.

That's why a musician doesn't wait for inspiration. They sit down at the piano and play scales for two minutes. Not a concert, not a composition, just simple notes. The act of beginning pulls them into the work. The resistance shrinks. The denominator collapses. Soon, they're improvising. Then creating. The equation tipped the second they touched the keys.

It works in business too. A small business owner spent months stuck in branding hell—fonts, websites, color palettes, mission statements. He had value and expectancy; he knew the business mattered and he believed he could pull it off. But delay was enormous. He hadn't spoken to a single customer. Then he forced himself to send one cold email. Just one. A stranger replied. The business was real now. He wasn't waiting for a customer. He had one. His motivation tripled because the timeline collapsed from someday to now.

Athletes know this better than anyone. Kobe Bryant was famous for starting his workouts at four in the morning. Not because he loved waking up early, but because he knew that once he was moving, the inertia carried him. By starting before the world woke up, he collapsed delay to zero. He wasn't someone waiting to get better at basketball. He was already getting better, before sunrise. The denominator was gone, and that math gave him a career defined by relentless momentum.

But you don't need to be Kobe or a founder to prove the point. Sam, worked as an insurance adjuster. Every day he stared at a backlog of files that seemed endless. For weeks he told himself he'd clear them when he had a big block of time. That block never came. One morning, overwhelmed, he whispered to himself, "One claim." That was it. He opened one file, processed it, and closed it. The relief was instant. He wasn't drowning anymore. He wasn't behind on everything. He was a man who had completed a claim. So he opened another. Then another. By lunch, he'd done more work than the previous three days combined. The difference wasn't energy or skill. It was the denominator collapsing. Delay was gone because he was already in motion.

The same principle shows up in the workplace. Psychologist

Teresa Amabile from Harvard ran a landmark study tracking employees' daily diaries across multiple industries. She found that the single biggest factor driving motivation at work wasn't bonuses, recognition, or even purpose. It was the "progress principle"—the sense of making tangible forward motion on meaningful tasks. Employees reported feeling most engaged and motivated on the days they made even small progress, like closing one case or finishing one section of a report. In other words, motivation wasn't tied to finishing the project, but to collapsing the delay with visible starts. The smallest wins tipped the entire equation.

This isn't about heroics. It's about leverage. If you're idle, delay stretches, impulsiveness rises, expectancy drops, value feels distant. The equation works against you. But once you start— even badly—you shrink the denominator and bump the numerator. You believe a little more because you've got proof. You value the work more because you're in it. The entire equation tips with one move.

Waiting feels safer, but waiting is the trap. People say they're gathering more information, waiting for the right season, trying to get motivated. What they're really doing is living in the worst possible zone of the math—high delay, high impulsiveness, low movement. Killing their own momentum by refusing to just start. Starting isn't just action. It's a reframe of identity. You're no longer someone thinking about the thing. You're the person doing it. That identity shift fuels expectancy, which multiplies motivation further.

It's inertia in real life. Objects at rest stay at rest. Objects in motion stay in motion. Your body, your brain, your business— they're all subject to the same law. Once you've begun, even awkwardly, you're carried forward. The denominator has been killed. The math is yours again.

This is why the turning points in life rarely come from breakthroughs or epiphanies. They come from inconvenient starts. The shaky first draft. The embarrassing first video. The late-night email to a trainer. The terrifying first cold call. None of those look like much from the outside. But in the equation, they're denominator killers. They're everything.

If you understand this, you stop asking, "How do I get motivated?" and you start asking, "What's the smallest start I can make right now?" You collapse the delay. You cut impulsiveness off at the knees. You give yourself proof. The motivation comes after.

That's why I use start lists instead of to-do lists. A to-do list is pressure and guilt. A start list is math. A handful of things I'm willing to begin, not finish. Once I start, the equation tilts, and the rest usually follows. This isn't semantics. It's strategy.

Motivation doesn't live in the finish line. It lives in the start. Begin, and you change the math. Begin again, and you build a rhythm. And if you keep collapsing delay, you stop needing motivation altogether. You're not waiting anymore. You're already in motion.

Chapter 41 — Start Signals to Maintain Focus

Starting is a skill. Focus is a practice.

At the beginning of any effort, focus feels effortless. Energy is high. The task feels new. Attention cooperates. But that phase is short-lived. The real challenge begins when novelty disappears and the work turns quiet, repetitive, or unclear. That's when focus starts to leak.

This chapter isn't about getting started. It's about staying oriented once you're underway.

Start Signals don't stop working after ignition—they change roles. Early on, they push you into motion. Later, they act as navigational aids. They don't add energy. They prevent drift.

The modern environment makes sustained focus unnatural. Notifications, tabs, ambient urgency, and internal noise constantly pull attention sideways. The problem isn't distraction itself—it's uncorrected drift. Most people don't notice when their attention slides off task. They feel busy, but they're no longer pointed at the work.

This is where a focus signal earns its keep.

A focus signal is not a rule and not a reprimand. It's a directional cue. It doesn't say "work harder." It says "come back." The moment your mind starts negotiating—email, research, tweaking, checking—you deploy the signal and realign.

Think of attention like a beam. Without correction, it naturally wanders. A signal narrows it again.

For example, when perfectionism creeps in, the signal "Keep it ugly" cuts off over-editing. When overthinking slows progress, "Just the next brick" returns attention to execution. When comparison pulls your eyes outward, "Eyes on your own lane" brings them back to the task at hand. These signals don't suppress thought. They redirect it.

Focus isn't a locked state. It's a repeated act of return.

During deep work—writing, problem-solving, building—feedback is delayed. That delay invites doubt. The signal bridges that gap. It keeps attention local. Hands on the work. Eyes on the page. One window, one task.

I've relied on this in my own writing. Not to force productivity, but to prevent wandering. When attention started slipping, the signal didn't motivate me—it oriented me. It kept me close enough to the work for momentum to reestablish itself.

This is the mistake people make: they treat focus as a feeling when it's really a behavioral alignment, and the signal is what makes that alignment repeatable. Rules say "don't get distracted," while signals say "back to the page," because rules create tension and signals create continuity. The goal isn't perfect concentration but fast correction—drift is inevitable, direction is optional—and starting gets you moving while focus keeps you pointed.

Chapter 42 — The Recovery Advantage

Starting is a skill. Staying in the game is an advantage.

Everyone drifts. The difference isn't who loses focus—it's who recovers fastest.

Most people think consistency comes from discipline. It doesn't. It comes from recovery speed. The faster you return to the work after disruption, the more output you accumulate over time. Delay is the real enemy.

This chapter isn't about focus itself. It's about what happens after focus breaks.

Attention follows a predictable loop: engagement, resistance, drift, recovery, reentry. Nearly everyone fails at recovery. They drift, notice it, feel frustration or guilt, and stall. That stall compounds. Minutes turn into hours. Hours turn into abandonment.

Recovery is the leverage point.

Start Signals evolve here. They stop acting as steering tools and become reentry triggers. Their job is not to hold attention—it's to collapse the gap between noticing drift and returning to action.

That gap is where most progress dies.

Neuroscience backs this up. High performers aren't immune to distraction. Their minds wander just as often as everyone else's.

What separates them is how quickly they come back. Each successful reentry strengthens the circuit. Recovery becomes reflex.

This is why recovery beats discipline. Discipline tries to prevent drift. Recovery assumes drift and trains return.

A recovery signal doesn't argue with your mind. It doesn't shame you for leaving. It simply marks the moment of return. "Back to it." "Here again." "Hands on."

In my own work, this mattered more than motivation. On days when energy was low and quitting felt reasonable, the signal didn't inspire me. It shortened the pause. It brought me back before resistance could solidify into avoidance.

Flow doesn't come first. Reentry does.

People wait to "feel focused" before resuming. That's backward. Elite performers resume first. Focus follows action, not the other way around.

This is why recovery compounds. Every quick return saves time. Every saved minute compounds into hours. Over weeks and months, that advantage becomes massive.

Rules say "don't get distracted," while signals say "return now," because rules judge failure and signals normalize it. The goal isn't zero drift but zero delay, and once you've built the signal that starts the fire, you build the one that pulls you back when it flickers—write it down, keep it visible, make it the phrase you trust when your mind offers exits, because starting gets you in the game and recovery is what keeps you winning.

Chapter 43 — Integrating Start Cells into Daily Routines

A Start Cell is built from three simple parts: time, action, and a Start Signal. By now you know what each means. Time is the anchor. Action is the first step. The Start Signal is the phrase that cuts through resistance. That's the structure. But knowing it is not enough. To make it work, you have to install Start Cells into your daily routine. Not once in a while. Not when you feel like it. Every single day, until they become automatic.

People often wait for the perfect day, the right moment, or some extra burst of motivation. That delay is where progress dies. You don't need the perfect day. You need a repeatable routine where the start is guaranteed. A Start Cell isn't a theory. It's a system. And systems only work if they're applied consistently.

Routines are the ground you stand on. We like to imagine that when life tests us, we'll rise to the occasion. That's a nice story. In truth, you don't rise to the occasion—you fall to the level of your routines. If those routines are loose, you'll collapse when pressure hits. If they're solid, you'll perform without hesitation. That's why Start Cells must be integrated into daily life. They give your routines the structure to hold under stress.

One start is a spark. Repeated starts are fuel. A single action may shift the needle for a moment, but it won't change your trajectory. The compounding effect comes from repetition. It comes from starting again and again until it is no longer a decision. The daily presence of Start Cells creates momentum that doesn't fade overnight. It turns starting into identity.

Most people think they need motivation. That's a mistake. Motivation is unreliable. It's inconsistent, emotional, and usually absent when you need it most. What you need is structure. A Start Cell is structure disguised as simplicity. It doesn't ask how you feel. It doesn't care about your mood. It tells you: at this time, with this cue, you take this action. Resistance has no room to negotiate because the action has already been decided.

This is why routines are not just helpful—they are non-negotiable. When you embed a Start Cell into your morning, your work block, and your evening, you remove the biggest drag on progress: hesitation. You no longer wonder if you'll begin. You begin because the system demands it.

Let's make this concrete with some micro examples. In the morning: place your tools where they'll meet you the moment you wake. A yoga mat, dumbbells, or even a notebook on the desk. The Start Signal is "begin." The action is stepping into the cue before thought interferes.

At midday: when your focus starts to break and you feel the pull of distraction, the Start Cell is five minutes on the hard project instead of scrolling. The Start Signal is "just five." The action is opening the file and writing the first line, or dialing the first number. That's enough to break resistance.

In the evening: set out tomorrow's tools before bed. Start Signal: "I'm ready." Action: ten seconds of prep so the next morning starts clean. It's a small gesture, but it closes the loop and sets up the next cell.

Notice how small these are. That's the power. Start Cells don't require a grand ritual or massive time commitment. They're compact and specific. Which is why they stick. Complexity kills routines. Simplicity protects them.

When I committed to improving my fitness, I didn't build it around a detailed gym plan or wait for the perfect schedule. I built a Start Cell into my mornings. A yoga mat, two dumbbells, exercise bands, and a pair of vice grips sat in the corner of the room. That was it. No setup required, no decisions to make. The Start Signal was "begin." Most mornings I started with my eyes half closed. But the tools were waiting, and the Start Cell carried me into motion before my brain could talk me out of it. Over time it became routine. I no longer asked if I would exercise. I simply began.

The same principle carried into writing. At first, the idea of producing chapters felt overwhelming. The scope was too large, the resistance too strong. So I stripped it down to a Start Cell: sit at the desk at the same time each morning and write one paragraph. Just one. The Start Signal was "just begin." Some days that was all I managed. Most days, once the paragraph was written, momentum carried me further. The pages stacked. The chapters formed. What once felt impossible turned into steady progress, built paragraph by paragraph.

Stephen King takes this principle to scale. People imagine a writer waiting for inspiration. King doesn't work that way. His Start Cell is simple and disciplined: sit down every morning and write 2,000 words. No questions, no negotiation. He doesn't wonder whether ideas will come—he begins. That daily routine has carried him through decades of work and dozens of bestsellers. His success is not the product of waiting for inspiration, but of embedding a Start Cell into his mornings that never breaks.

Ivan Lendl dominated men's tennis through the 1980s. He wasn't flashy or emotional; he was methodical, disciplined, and brutally consistent. Eight Grand Slam titles, nineteen finals, and 270 weeks at No. 1—built on routine, not adrenaline. His Start Cell was microscopic: the first exact, mechanical stroke in warm-up. Same angle, same tempo, same footwork, every day. That tiny ignition flipped him from human to machine. It wasn't motivation or drama. It was embedding the start so deeply that skipping it felt unnatural. Once he hit that first clean ball, the rest of the day was already decided.

Beethoven had his own version. He was obsessive about his morning routine. Every day he brewed coffee with exactly sixty beans and then sat down to compose. That was his Start Cell. Time: morning. Action: sit at the piano. Start Signal: unspoken but clear—"begin." The routine was so rigid that even when inspiration was low, music still emerged. The consistency mattered more than the mood.

And it's not just the famous. A design student struggled with procrastination on building a portfolio. Weeks passed with nothing finished. She finally set a rule: before bed each night, she would open her sketchbook and draw one line. Just one. The Start Signal was "mark the page." Most nights she drew more, but even the minimum kept her connected to the work. Months later she had a complete portfolio—and more importantly, the identity of a creator, not a procrastinator.

Science confirms what these stories illustrate. Habits don't stick because of motivation. They stick because they're repeated against a stable cue until they become automatic. Phillippa Lally's study at University College London tracked people forming new habits and found it took an average of 66 days before the behavior felt natural. Some locked in sooner, others much later, but the lesson was clear: automaticity comes from repetition, not inspiration. A Start Cell gives you that repeatable entry point so the loop has a chance to harden.

There's another piece here—decision fatigue. Roy Baumeister's research showed that the brain's ability to make choices depletes over the day. That's why diets collapse at night, why hard work stalls in the afternoon, why most people cave on the very things they swore they'd do. Every decision burns energy. A Start Cell removes that burn. It pre-decides the start. At this time, with this cue, you take this action. The negotiation is gone, which means the energy remains for doing.

Peter Gollwitzer's work on implementation intentions adds another layer. He showed that people who set "if-then" plans ("If it's 7 a.m., then I'll run." "If I sit at my desk, then I'll write a paragraph.") were far more likely to follow through. That's exactly what a Start Cell is—an if-then stripped to its essentials. Time, action, Start Signal. Simple enough to repeat, strong enough to survive resistance.

So how do you install these into daily life? Start simple. Don't try to overhaul your entire schedule at once. Pick three points in your day—morning, work block, evening. Attach one Start Cell to each.

In the morning: choose one action that sets the tone. It could be writing a paragraph, stretching, or simply drinking water before coffee. Anchor it to waking up. That's your first cell.

In your work block: identify the hardest task. Then break it into the smallest possible start. Open the document. Write the first sentence. Make the first call. Start Signal: "begin." That's your second cell.

In the evening: prepare the next day. Lay out clothes, set up tools, write down the next morning's first action. Start Signal: "tomorrow is ready." That's your third cell.

Three Start Cells are enough to reshape a day. More is not better. Complexity will make you quit. Three is manageable. Three will hold.

Here's the truth: you will miss some. That's inevitable. The mistake is thinking that missing one ruins the system. It doesn't. The point of Start Cells is that they are modular. Miss the morning? Start at midday. Miss midday? Lock in the evening. The rule is simple: start again at the next block. No guilt, no spiral, just reset. That is how you beat perfectionism.

Over time, these small actions accumulate into something bigger. They become proof that you can start, no matter the day, no matter the mood. And once you've built that proof, you've built momentum. The identity shift happens quietly. You stop being the person who sometimes begins and become the person who always begins. That identity doesn't break easily.

This is how routines become strength. They don't just guide your day—they define you. Integrating Start Cells into daily routines means that starting is no longer a question. It's not optional. It's automatic. That's the point.

So here's your challenge. Pick three Start Cells right now. One for morning, one for work, one for evening. Make them simple. Anchor them to clear cues. Write your Start Signals. Practice them for seven days. Don't wait for the perfect schedule. Don't negotiate with mood. Just start. Then start again. And again. That's how routines harden into identity. That's how you carry momentum that doesn't break when life pushes back. That's how you integrate Start Cells into daily life until starting is who you are.

Chapter 44 — Time the Flame, Not the Spark

You don't time the match. You time the burn.

You don't need a timer to strike a match. That's the spark—the starting moment. It happens in a second, and that second is sacred. But the burn is different. The burn is where the work happens, where heat turns to progress. That's what needs timing. Most people confuse the two. They obsess over planning the strike, over-measuring it, over-analyzing whether the match will light. And then they finally start—and drift. The flame flickers, fades, or turns to smoke.

Starting isn't enough when the task is long, dull, or draining. You have to time the flame.

You've probably felt this before. You start writing, editing, or cleaning your inbox. You follow the Start Cell framework. You move. You light the match. But five minutes later, the flame weakens. Notifications, doubt, hunger, or "let me just check one thing" slip in—and the fire goes out. Distraction thrives on open-ended time. When there's no frame, no edge, no promise, you're floating. Drifting. Thinking instead of doing.

Put a clock on it and everything changes. Not forever. Not an hour. Not some perfect block on your calendar. Just a pulse, a bracket, a vow. "For the next seventeen minutes, this is all I do." No excuses, no breaks, no scrolling—just burn.

You don't need a perfect number. The point isn't precision; it's containment. The brain handles effort differently when it knows the pain has an endpoint. Suddenly you don't need willpower—you have a container. You're no longer pushing against infinity. You're holding the flame until the bell rings.

Not every task deserves a timer. You don't time your deep conversations or your prayers. You don't time a hike, a dinner, or a moment of love. But you do time the friction tasks—the ones that stall you, scatter you, or drain your will. Writing a tough section? Timer. Making prospecting calls? Timer. Reading boring material or organizing files? Timer. Not because you're racing, but because you're respecting the flame.

Timing a task is a promise, not a prison. You're telling your mind, "We're not escaping. We're not chasing dopamine. We're doing this—fully—for fifteen minutes." It's not about tracking. It's about commitment. Most people start without a frame or a vow. They strike the match, admire the light, and forget to feed it. Then they say things like, "I started writing last week but didn't stick with it," or "I showed up to the gym but just wandered around." That's not a starting problem. It's a burning problem. The fix isn't more hustle—it's better timing.

You don't need an app or a productivity system. Just decide in the moment: "This task gets eighteen minutes. No more, no less." Use your phone, your stove, or a sand timer if you want. But once it's set, don't check the time halfway through—that's cheating. Trust the fire to run its course.

Something happens inside that window. Resistance starts to fade. Your brain quiets down. The task becomes the room you live in. It's not always pleasant, but it's present. And when the bell rings, you stop—or you keep going—but either way, you've burned clean. You didn't waste an hour half-working.

You gave eighteen minutes of full fire.

That's the difference.

You don't need to time everything. If you over-time your life, it becomes another form of control—a cage. This isn't about micromanaging every breath. It's about learning when a task needs help. And when it does, give it a frame. Give it a flame.

Some people avoid timing because they're afraid of what they'll see. They're scared to face what actually happens when they sit and work. But that's exactly why they should do it. Inside that burn window lives the version of you that gets things done. Not perfectly. Not permanently. But honestly. That's what matters.

If you want to ritualize it, fine—light a candle, close your tabs, put on a track that lasts as long as your timer—but don't wait to feel ready. Start. Set the time. Burn. You don't time the match; you time the burn. You start without fear, burn with boundaries, and exit with clarity.

Chapter 45 — The Start Chain

A Start Cell is one decisive move. It cuts through hesitation and gets you moving. But one start by itself can also fizzle. You can begin, then stall. A spark without fuel dies out. That's where the Start Chain comes in.

A Start Chain is a series of linked starts. Instead of treating each action as separate, you connect them so one leads naturally into the next. The result is rhythm. The sequence keeps you moving when motivation is low, when distraction calls, and when pressure is high. Chains create continuity. They remove the constant friction of deciding "what next?" Once you're in motion, the chain carries you. And because each step is already scripted, you don't waste energy on choices—you simply move forward.

Chains matter because they protect you from stalling. Starting once is progress, but it's fragile. You can stop at any moment. A chain adds weight. Break one link, and you feel the loss of the whole. That sense of continuity gives you leverage. Chains also multiply energy. Each completed action lowers resistance for the next. You don't have to fire yourself up multiple times. You just step into the chain, and the sequence takes over. What feels impossible as a whole becomes manageable in parts.

The best football coaches understand this principle. They don't walk into a game hoping their team will improvise the right moves in the opening minutes. They script them. The first ten plays are decided before kickoff. Everyone on the team knows what's coming. The quarterback knows. The line knows. The receivers know. Those opening plays are a chain. One play sets up the next. Nobody hesitates. Nobody debates. They execute.

By the time the script runs, the team has rhythm and confidence. They're in the game, not trying to get into the game. Great coaches leave room for one or two audibles if the defense surprises them, but the core chain is non-negotiable. That opening script builds momentum and sets the tone.

You can apply the same principle in your own life. Script the first ten minutes of your morning. Script the first three steps of your work block. Don't leave them to chance or wait for inspiration. Build a Start Chain and let the structure carry you into motion before resistance has time to regroup.

One of the clearest places to apply a Start Chain is in work. It's easy to get trapped in distraction—emails, notifications, small tasks that feel busy but accomplish nothing. A chain stops that drift. I built a sequence for my mornings: open the calendar, send one priority email, then open the critical project file. That was it. Three steps, clear and simple. The first step was too small to resist. Once I opened the calendar, the next link followed naturally. By the time I reached the project file, I was already working. I didn't wander into productivity—I entered it through the chain. The chain didn't make the work effortless. Hard tasks were still hard. But the hesitation that usually slowed me down was gone. Instead of circling around the work, I was inside it before I had time to stall.

In 1928, psychologist Maria Ovsiankina made a discovery that explains why Start Chains work. She gave people small tasks—puzzles, writing exercises, simple problems—and then interrupted them before they were finished. What she found was surprising. Most participants returned to the tasks on their own, even when they didn't have to. They felt compelled to complete what was unfinished. This became known as the Ovsiankina Effect. It expands on the earlier Zeigarnik Effect, which showed that people remember incomplete tasks more vividly than finished ones. Ovsiankina proved something more: unfinished tasks create tension that pushes us to resume them.

That is the psychology behind a Start Chain. Once you open the first link, the brain wants to finish the sequence. An incomplete chain pulls you forward. You don't have to force motivation—your mind resists leaving the job undone. This is why chains are more powerful than isolated starts. A single start can be abandoned. A chain creates its own gravity. Break it, and you feel the weight of the interruption. Keep it, and momentum builds with less effort.

Start simple. Identify two or three small actions you can link together. Don't try to build a long sequence immediately. Complexity kills consistency. Begin with a short chain you can repeat daily. For example: Morning—wake up → drink water → stretch. Work—open calendar → send one priority email → open project file. Evening—put away phone → write tomorrow's first action → lights out. Each step is small, but together they create continuity. You don't finish the first step and wonder what to do next. The next link is already in place.

As you repeat, the chain becomes self-reinforcing. One day of continuity leads to another. The Ovsiankina pull strengthens. Breaking the chain feels wrong. Protecting it feels natural. Chains are strong, but they are also fragile if ignored. Protect them deliberately. Mark completions on a calendar. Track your sequence in a notebook. Seeing continuity builds pride and commitment. This is why streak-tracking works—it makes the chain visible.

Here's the crucial rule: if one link breaks, don't let the whole chain collapse. Reset at the next cue. The chain doesn't die because you missed a link. It survives if you restart quickly. Remember, the brain hates unfinished work. If you leave the chain open, that unfinished-task pull will push you to resume. Use that. Let the tension pull you back in, and the continuity will hold.

A Start Cell proves you can begin. A Start Chain proves you can continue. One start is strength. A chain of starts is momentum. Don't leave your day to improvisation. Script the first moves. Build the links. Protect the continuity. Once you enter the chain, the sequence itself will carry you. The strongest performers, the sharpest systems, and the most disciplined routines aren't accidents. They are chains—linked starts that eliminate hesitation, multiply energy, and create momentum that lasts. Build your chain. Defend it. Let it define you.

Chapter 46 — How to Do Boring Like a Wild Achiever

Let's get something straight: this chapter isn't about inbox zero or vacuuming the truck. It was forged for bold beginnings—for dream ignitions. For the projects you've put off. The business idea. The new path. That next book. But here's the twist: if you want to build the habit of powerful starts, you need reps. Even on the small stuff.

That's where boring tasks come in. Not because they matter on their own, but because they keep your ignition system sharp. Boring tasks are like daily drills for a professional athlete. No crowd. No spotlight. Just reps. But when the moment comes, you're ready.

Think of a soldier field-stripping their weapon. Or a pianist doing finger warm-ups before a concert. It's not glamorous. But it's what sharpens the edge. It's what makes the real thing flow. Starting something dull is a low-risk way to practice ignition when your brain wants to avoid it. And if you can win the small battles, you've already trained for the big ones.

Let's say your inbox is flooded. You don't want to clean it. It feels useless, endless. But if you tell yourself, "This is just me sharpening the tool," something changes. You stop fighting the task and just start. You remind your body that it knows how to move.

Each boring task becomes a rep at the mental gym. That's not a metaphor—it's neurobiology. Your brain forms habits and mental shortcuts based on action, not theory. When you act without drama, you're rewiring your start mechanism. You're creating a neural shortcut that says: I can begin—even when I don't want to.

And here's what most people don't realize: when it comes time to make a real move—a conversation, a pitch, a chapter, a risk—your ignition muscle is already warm. Your body and brain know how to begin. The start no longer feels like a cliff. It's just one more step.

I once cleared out 2,000 emails in a single sitting. Not because I suddenly loved Gmail. But because I told myself, "This is sharpening the blade." I started. It cascaded. I ended up clearing the inbox, organizing files, even writing a new pitch email that landed a meeting. Momentum doesn't ask for meaning. It creates it.

Contrast that with a friend who kept saying he needed to organize his files. Every time he thought about it, he got overwhelmed. Instead of starting, he'd research productivity apps or read blog posts about digital clutter. He never made progress, because he never crossed the line into motion. He thought clarity had to come first. But the truth is, clarity is often on the other side of a small, boring start.

The difference between us wasn't intelligence or discipline. It was ignition. I started. He didn't.

That's why boring tasks matter. Not for the tasks themselves, but for the trust they build. Every time you act without overthinking, you're creating proof: I can start. And the brain remembers that. It stores it. The next time resistance shows up, your brain doesn't panic. It knows the way forward. You've practiced it.

And there's science behind it. In a 2012 study by Dr. Roy Baumeister on ego depletion, researchers found that the ability to exert self-control and start small tasks consistently built a higher baseline of mental resilience. In plain English: people who got in the habit of doing boring but necessary things were better equipped for the real challenges. They could handle more friction, more resistance, more pressure. Starting small made them mentally tougher.

You can use this principle in every domain. Let's say you've been avoiding calling five clients back. It's not strategic avoidance—it's just dread. Pick the lowest-friction task: return one voicemail. That's the start. The rest often follows. You're not doing busywork. You're priming your ignition system.

I've even used this mindset to reframe tasks I once dreaded. Updating old listings. Reviewing contracts. Organizing receipts. Not because I enjoy it—but because I enjoy who I become when I can start without delay. I want to be the guy who can initiate anything—creative or boring—without mental struggle. That's what separates pros from dabblers.

Boring work doesn't slow you down. It sharpens your blade. Boring tasks are your test lab. Your dojo. You practice presence, clarity, and precision. You reduce drag. You separate emotional weight from physical action. You learn to move without overthinking. And when you do that often enough, you build something very rare: automatic ignition. No need for motivation. No need for permission. Just movement.

Here's the magic: once you've mastered boring, hard things

become easier. Because you've proven you can start even when you don't feel like it. And that's the gateway to wild achievement. No more internal negotiations. No more excuses disguised as planning.

Don't romanticize boredom. Just start it. One drawer. One email. One phone call. One small step that builds the wiring you'll need when it's time to launch something real.

Tell yourself this: "This isn't maintenance. This is ignition training." That mindset alone puts you ahead of almost everyone, because while most people wait for inspiration, you're building something stronger. If you can start the boring things, you can start the real things—that's how you train ignition, how you rewire belief, and why you move now rather than later.

PART V — The Inner Game of Starting

Chapter 47 — Start Again Tomorrow

No matter how disciplined you are, you will miss. The system will break. A chain will snap. A day will slip. This isn't a possibility—it's a certainty. The test isn't whether you keep a perfect streak. The test is what you do the day after you fall. The answer is simple: start again tomorrow.

That's the principle that separates progress from collapse. Perfection is brittle. One crack and it shatters. Resilience is durable. It bends and resets. If you make "start again tomorrow" a rule, no lapse can take you out of the game.

When people fail, it isn't the single miss that destroys them. It's the story they tell themselves afterward. They miss one workout, and instead of restarting, they decide they've blown it. They skip one day of writing, and instead of returning the next morning, they declare themselves blocked. The setback isn't the problem. Quitting is the problem. Starting again tomorrow cuts off that spiral. It reframes failure as interruption, not identity. It says: today was lost, but tomorrow is open. The chain is intact if I reset.

Fitness: you miss a workout. Tomorrow, back on the mat. No double session to punish yourself. No guilt. Just the next set at the usual time.

Work: distraction eats your day. Tomorrow, start with the first three links of your chain—calendar, priority email, project file. The system restarts itself.

Writing: you skip a day. Tomorrow, return to the smallest unit: one paragraph. Not a marathon catch-up. One link, one restart.

Each example shows the same truth. The habit isn't about never missing. The habit is about resuming.

When I first built a routine around writing, I slipped often. Some days, life pulled me away before I could get to the desk. In the past, that would have ended the streak. I would have told myself I'd failed and let weeks pass. This time, I changed the rule. If I missed today, I would return tomorrow, no matter what. And I would return to the smallest unit: one paragraph. That was the contract.

Over time, that single adjustment made all the difference. Misses still happened. But they no longer expanded into gaps. They shrank into single days. The routine lived because I always restarted. The identity shifted from "someone who tries" to "someone who always comes back."

Psychology backs up the principle of starting again tomorrow. Two key insights explain why.

First, Kristin Neff's research on self-compassion shows that people who forgive themselves for setbacks recover faster than those who punish themselves. In one study, participants who practiced self-compassion after breaking a diet were far more likely to return to healthy eating than those who responded with guilt or self-criticism. The lesson is clear: shame and punishment extend failure. Self-compassion shortens it. The fastest way back into momentum is not beating yourself up, but calmly resetting and beginning again.

Second, Altmann and Trafton's work on "resumption lag" demonstrates that people re-engage with interrupted tasks more quickly when they have a clear re-entry point. If you leave a task mid-sentence, you return faster. If you mark exactly where to restart, the gap between stopping and resuming shrinks dramatically. Applied to daily routines, this means the best way to recover after a miss is to know the precise next step. Not "get back in shape." Not "catch up on all the writing I missed." Just: tomorrow, one set. Tomorrow, one paragraph. The reset point is what collapses hesitation.

Together these studies prove that resilience isn't luck. It's structure. Forgive yourself, define the re-entry, and the system pulls you forward. That's the essence of starting again tomorrow.

Define the reset point. If you miss, know exactly what tomorrow looks like. The smallest unit is best—one set, one email, one paragraph.
Don't make up. Never double the work to "catch up." It creates overwhelm and sets up failure. The chain resumes from tomorrow's link, not yesterday's backlog.
Restart quickly. The faster you reset, the less damage the miss does. A one-day gap is harmless. A one-week gap is dangerous.
Build identity. Don't define yourself as someone who never misses. Define yourself as someone who always restarts. That identity survives any interruption.

The point is not perfection. The point is persistence. The system is not about streaks that never break. It's about streaks that restart every time they do. If you build this rule into your life—start again tomorrow—nothing can permanently stop you. Setbacks shrink to their real size: small, temporary, recoverable. The chain survives because you repair it the next morning.

This is not weakness; it's the strongest discipline there is, because no matter how many times resistance knocks you down, you return and begin again. That's what separates those who drift from those who move forward—not the absence of failure, but the presence of one unbreakable habit: starting again tomorrow.

Chapter 48 — What to Start When You are Lost

There are seasons when direction disappears. You feel adrift, unsure of where to go next. The path you thought you were on is gone, or you don't even see a path at all. You wake up and realize you're moving but not progressing, busy but not advancing. That feeling of being lost is more common than people admit. And in those moments, the temptation is to wait. To pause until clarity returns. To hold off until you know the "right" move. That is the mistake. Waiting deepens the fog. The longer you stay still, the heavier confusion becomes. The way out is not to think harder or analyze more. The way out is to start.

When you are lost, don't look for the perfect start. Look for any start.

Clarity doesn't create action. Action creates clarity. The illusion is that if you could only see the map, then you would know where to go. But the map appears only after you begin moving. Think of standing in a dark room with a flashlight. You can't see the entire space. But take one step, move the beam, and the next part of the floor is revealed. That's how it works when you're lost. One start shines light on the next.

This is why starting matters more than planning in moments of confusion. The start breaks inertia. It generates information. It reveals what was hidden. The simple act of motion tells you more than hours of speculation.

When you don't know what to start, default to these three

anchors.

Start with health. When direction is unclear, return to the body. Move. Stretch. Walk. Breathe. Eat clean food. Health is always a foundation. Improving it is never wasted. And the act of strengthening the body often clears the mind.

Start with the work at hand. Look at your desk, your room, your immediate surroundings. Choose one small task in front of you. Reply to one message. Organize one drawer. Pay one bill. Action in the smallest circle builds momentum that spreads outward.

Start with service. If you cannot find purpose for yourself, help someone else. Call a friend. Assist a colleague. Volunteer a small act of support. Service pulls you out of your head and reconnects you to value. Direction often returns when you see that your effort still matters to others.

Any of these three domains—health, work, service—can act as the first stone in the path. You don't need all of them. One is enough.

There was a time I felt overwhelmed by competing demands. Too many projects, none of them clear. Every decision felt like the wrong one. Instead of untangling the whole knot, I returned to the smallest unit. I put down a yoga mat and moved for fifteen minutes. Nothing strategic, nothing planned. Just motion. That start shifted something. The workout gave me energy, and the energy gave me focus. From there, I sat down and wrote a paragraph. One action opened the door to another. By the end of the day, the fog wasn't gone, but it was thinner. The path had begun to reappear. The key wasn't clarity. The key was action.

Karl Weick, a researcher who studied how organizations deal with uncertainty, coined the term "sensemaking." His insight was blunt: people don't figure things out by thinking first and acting second. They act first, then interpret. Weick put it this way: "How can I know what I think until I see what I do?"

This is the psychology of starting when you are lost. You can't reason your way out of confusion from a standstill. But when you take action—even a small one—you create data. You give yourself something to interpret. Movement generates feedback, and feedback generates direction. It's not the analysis that rescues you. It's the act. The sense comes after.

When you feel lost, don't demand a perfect plan. Use a reset method. Choose a domain. Pick health, work, or service. Don't overthink it. Any of them will work. Define one action. The smallest possible unit: walk for ten minutes, answer one email, call one person. Complete and observe. Do it fully. Then notice what follows. Often the next action appears. Let momentum guide. Don't map the whole day. Map the next link. The path is revealed by walking it.

Lost is a feeling, not a fate. Stagnation makes it permanent. Motion makes it temporary. When you don't know what to do, start with something simple. Strengthen your body, clear your immediate work, or serve someone else. The direction will emerge once you are moving.

The greatest trap is believing you need clarity to act, when the truth is the opposite: you need action to find clarity. So when you're lost, don't freeze or wait for the perfect path—start anywhere, start small, start today, and tomorrow the road will be clearer because you moved.

Chapter 49 — Keep the Start Sacred

The start is not just another part of the day. It's not interchangeable with errands, messages, or casual busywork. The start is sacred. It's the ignition point that carries everything else. If you weaken it, the system weakens. If you protect it, the system becomes unshakable. Sacred means untouchable. It means non-negotiable. It means you don't bargain with it, excuse it, or let it slip behind things that matter less. When you keep the start sacred, you protect the one ritual that makes everything else possible.

People fail because they treat the start as optional, something they can push back or squeeze in around the edges. When they do, life swallows it whole. The day fills with noise, energy scatters, and the chance to build momentum disappears. You don't control your whole day—emergencies show up, people need you, distractions multiply. But you can control one thing: the start. If you keep it sacred, you anchor everything.

Sacred is not just about religion in the formal sense. It's about treating the start with reverence, as if it carries weight beyond itself. Think about how you treat an important appointment. You don't cancel lightly. You don't let small interruptions override it. You prepare, you show up, and you respect the time. That's what sacred means. This isn't only about discipline. It's about the spiritual weight of vocation. If you think your life is only about material possessions, you'll eventually wander. You'll lose interest, chase the next shiny object, and hollow out your own work. Treating the start as sacred reminds you that your work matters not just for income or achievement but because it's tied to something larger. Your vocation is more than a job. It's the through-line of your life. Protecting the start

177

is how you protect that calling.

When the start is sacred, you strip away negotiation. You stop asking, Should I? You stop debating. You show up and begin. Negotiation drains energy. Sacredness eliminates it. And that changes everything, because willpower is weak and moods fluctuate. But sacred ritual outlasts mood. It says: no matter how I feel, I begin.

Writers have always treated their starts as sacred. Hemingway began at dawn. Maya Angelou rented a bare hotel room to separate herself from the noise of life, showing up each morning to write. Athletes do the same—NBA players at the free throw line, tennis champions bouncing the ball the same way before a serve, quarterbacks running the same pre-snap checks. These rituals are not superstition. They are sacred starts. They anchor the mind, block out noise, and signal: now it begins.

I've lived the difference. When I let my start get sloppy, I'd check messages before entering my writing block. By the time I sat down, the sacredness was gone, momentum diluted. Compare that to the times I treated the start as inviolable— timer set, whisper in place, action triggered immediately. No screens, no interruptions. The quality and depth of work that followed was night and day. Sacredness didn't just protect time. It protected meaning.

Sacredness has enemies. The first is distraction—a glance at your phone, a notification, a casual interruption. Each intrusion weakens the ritual. The second is compromise—the habit of telling yourself, I'll start after I clear these small things. Once you trade the sacred for the trivial, the start is gone. The third is availability—if you make yourself open to everyone before you begin, you'll never get there. The truth is that nothing in your environment will keep your start sacred for you. The world will always press in. People will fill your calendar. Distractions will beg for attention. Protecting the start is your job, and if you don't defend it, nobody else will.

Research confirms what creators and performers have always known. Francesca Gino and Michael Norton studied rituals and found they improve performance because they create a sense of control and reduce anxiety. In one experiment, participants did better on stressful tasks after completing a short ritual. In another, rituals helped people process grief more effectively. The content didn't matter—it was the protected repetition that gave the act power. This is exactly what a sacred start is. It's not casual. It's not random. It's a ritual that signals importance. By making the beginning sacred, you cut away noise, frame the act with meaning, and give your mind the structure it needs to enter fully.

To keep the start sacred, first define it: the time, the place, the action. It doesn't have to be grand, just clear. Maybe it's 7:00 AM at the desk with your laptop. Maybe it's stepping on the mat after work. Maybe it's ten minutes in the evening with a notebook. Then guard it. Treat it like a sacred appointment. No distractions, no messages, no excuses. If someone asks for that time, decline. If your phone buzzes, ignore it. If chores call, they wait. Sacred means protected. Reinforce it with ritual. Whisper your phrase. Open the same document. Step onto the same mat. Consistency strengthens sacredness. Each repetition deepens the groove. The start becomes something you don't think about—you just enter. And defend it daily. One broken start can turn into a pattern if you don't reset immediately. Sacred doesn't mean flawless; it means protected. If you miss, return quickly. The moment you honor the start again, the sacredness is restored.

You can't make your whole day sacred. Life is too messy for that. But you don't need to. Protecting the start is enough. The start sets the tone. Once the first move is solid, the rest of the day organizes around it. Miss it, and the day drifts. Keep it, and the day sharpens. Sacredness at the start creates ripple effects you can't get any other way.

The start is not casual. It's not optional. It's sacred. Treat it that way, and you gain a lever that moves everything else. Let it be cheapened by distraction or compromise, and the foundation of your work will weaken. This is as much about faith as it is about discipline. If you think your life is only about possessions or outcomes, you'll wander, lose interest, and chase the next shiny object. But if you see your work—your writing, your craft, your vocation—as a calling, then protecting the start is a spiritual act. It's how you honor the work itself. It's how you keep your life from being consumed by trivial noise.

You can't control chaos. You can't control outcomes. But you can control the first move. Keep it sacred. Guard it. Honor it. Repeat it. And when you do, you'll find that sacredness spills into everything else. Because the start is not just a tactic—it's your daily covenant with the life you're building. And remember—covenants aren't built on applause. They're built in silence. That's where we go next.

Chapter 50 — Start Without Applause

Most people want to start only when someone else is watching. They want recognition, approval, and validation before they move. But that need for applause is a trap. It's inconsistent, unreliable, and dangerous. If your ability to begin depends on someone else's recognition, you've already lost. The truth is, applause rarely shows up at the start. Nobody cheers the first draft. Nobody claps when you walk into an empty gym. Nobody celebrates the first cold call, the first email, or the first morning you lace up and run when it's still dark outside. The start is silent. And it has to be.

If you can't move in silence, you won't survive long enough to reach the noise. The applause, if it comes at all, only arrives after years of quiet work. Applause feels good. It scratches the itch for validation. But it comes with a cost: dependency. The more you crave it, the more you shape your work for recognition instead of for growth. You hesitate until someone notices you. You measure yourself by likes, claps, shares, or feedback. And when applause doesn't come, you collapse. This is why so many projects never leave the ground. People wait to be recognized first. They want the audience before they perform. But that's not how it works. Applause comes later—if it comes at all. The start belongs to you alone.

Every meaningful pursuit begins in obscurity. The gym at 6 AM is empty. The first draft has no readers. The first song is played to an empty room. By the time anyone notices, the discipline is already deep. This reality can feel harsh, but it's freeing. You don't have to wait for approval. You don't have to wonder if anyone will care. You just start. And if you can start without applause, you've already built an edge most people never touch.

Sometimes silence—even hostility—is the advantage. Look at sports. When an underdog team enters a rival's stadium, they don't get applause. They're met with jeers, boos, and noise designed to break their focus. Yet many times, that's when the underdog performs best. Without applause, there are no illusions, no ego boosts, no distractions. Just the game in front of them. Pure execution. The players know nobody is cheering for them. That clarity sharpens their edge. They aren't playing for approval; they're playing to win. The hostile stadium strips away the ego and forces pure focus.

That's exactly how you should treat your starts. Don't expect applause. Don't need approval. Silence—or even doubt from others—can be your advantage. If you can begin without recognition, you're free. You build resilience, clarity, and strength. And when applause finally comes, it won't own you. You'll already know how to perform without it.

When I began writing, there was no audience. No readers, no feedback, no applause. It was just me at a desk, typing into the void. If I had needed recognition to keep going, I would have stopped in the first week. But the act itself became the reward. The ritual of sitting down, whispering "Start anyway," and producing one clean sentence—that was enough. Later, when people began to notice, it felt different. Encouraging, yes, but fleeting. One person praises you, another criticizes you, and if you let those swings dictate your momentum, you're finished. The only safe ground was to begin for myself, not for anyone else. The applause was never the point. The start was.

The same principle applied in business. Early mornings of outreach, calls, building systems—nobody saw that. Nobody cared. But those were the starts that built the foundation. Recognition came later, and by then it didn't matter. The discipline was already in place.

Psychology explains why applause is a weak foundation. Edward Deci and Richard Ryan's Self-Determination Theory shows that motivation is strongest when it comes from within—driven by autonomy, mastery, and purpose. External rewards—praise, applause, even money—can boost performance for a while. But when they dominate, they erode intrinsic drive. In one classic study, children who loved drawing were rewarded for it. When the rewards stopped, many lost interest in drawing altogether. External applause had crowded out their natural motivation.

This is why people who start for recognition rarely last. The applause is never enough, or it fades, or it shifts. But those who start for autonomy, mastery, and purpose keep going, with or without applause. They don't need an audience because the act itself is the reward.

How do you build this ability to start without applause? Create private starts—routines no one sees, streaks you don't post, rituals that exist only for you. Keep proof of your starts in a notebook, not online. Make the validation internal. Use your Start Signal as an internal contract. When you whisper "Start anyway" or "One brick," you aren't performing for an audience. You're performing for yourself. Train yourself to love the act itself. Enjoy the rep, the sentence, the call. Applause may come later, but it should never be the fuel. And embrace the silence. When nobody notices, when nobody claps, when nobody cares—that's when you're training the purest form of resilience. That's when you're building a foundation applause can't touch.

Applause fades. Recognition shifts. The crowd cheers today and forgets tomorrow. If that's what you're chasing, you'll always be dependent, fragile, and pulled by noise you can't control. The start, done in silence, is different. It belongs to you. It builds strength that lasts. The athlete in the hostile stadium doesn't need cheers to play well. The writer at dawn doesn't need readers to write a page. The entrepreneur making the first call doesn't need an audience to build momentum.

You don't start for applause. You start because starting is who you are. Applause is extra. Applause is temporary. But the daily ritual of beginning—that is permanent, sacred, and yours alone. So start without applause. Start without recognition. Start without anyone watching. That is where real strength is built. And when the applause finally comes, you'll know it was never the reason you began.

Chapter 51 — You Don't Need a Study to Start

One of the easiest ways to stall is to hide behind research. People convince themselves they're preparing. They read another article, sign up for another course, watch more videos. It feels productive. It looks responsible. But it's still waiting. This is procrastination in a lab coat. Preparation without motion is just another excuse. You don't need peer-reviewed proof to take a step forward. You don't need a permission slip from experts. You don't need a study to start. You need ignition.

Every breakthrough in history began before the research was complete. Entrepreneurs launched businesses before the case studies existed. Athletes pushed the limits of training before exercise science caught up. Artists created movements before critics had a name for them. The pattern is always the same: action first, studies second.

When I decided to get my FAA Part 107 commercial drone license, I didn't sign up for a prep course. Most people buy one for around $300 and follow the four-week schedule. I didn't have that time. I'd already been flying drones as a hobby for over three years. I knew the important part—how to fly them safely and skillfully. What I needed was the credential that would let me fly commercially. For real estate, that's a game changer. Listings with aerial shots and flyovers stand out, and they open doors to sellers.

So I set a deadline: seven days. I pulled the FAA outline, gathered the raw material, studied the airspace rules and charts, and scheduled the test. It wasn't elegant, but it was focused. A week later, I passed. Not because I followed the official playbook. Not because I bought the course. But because I started.

The same thing happened in my real estate business. I needed an automated postcard system that would run off a Google Sheet. New listings, just solds—the bread and butter of staying visible in a farm. The problem was I had never studied Google Apps Script. I had some background in PHP and JavaScript, but nothing specific. Most people in my position would have signed up for a course or hired someone. I didn't have the luxury of waiting.

So I jumped in. I wrote code, broke it, fixed it, and broke it again. After a string of hiccups and late nights, I had the system working in less than two weeks. Now I can push a button and have postcards go out automatically. No course. No certificate. Just motion.

The same lesson showed up on the water. My boat's ignition failed, and the wiring was a disaster. Over the years, different mechanics had patched and spliced wires for bilge pumps, trolling motors, gauges—you name it. When I brought it to reputable shops, they all told me the same thing: it couldn't be fixed without replacing the entire wiring harness—thousands of dollars and weeks of downtime.

I decided to do it myself. Armed with a multimeter, wiring diagrams, and a steady pace, I spent Saturdays tracing wires one by one, cutting out splices, labeling, and rebuilding the ignition. Less than three weeks later, the mess was gone. The system was clean, organized, and running like new. None of these projects required a study. They required a start.

And here's the funny part: the science still agrees. Psychologists talk about "action bias"—our tendency to favor doing something over doing nothing, even when waiting might be safer. In soccer penalty-kick studies, goalkeepers almost always dive left or right, even though statistically the best choice is often to stay in the center. Why? Because standing still feels wrong. Doing something feels better. People would rather act and be wrong than freeze and be "right."

That instinct, when directed, is powerful. Action bias explains why motion beats research paralysis. Your brain would rather generate proof through action than sit with uncertainty. That's why you learn faster in motion than you ever could from endless preparation.

Waiting feels safe, but it kills momentum. Information without execution is entertainment. And there will always be another expert, another framework, another course telling you to pause until you're ready. But "ready" is a moving target. The only thing that makes you ready is beginning.

So strip it down. Decide the action. Put a deadline on it. Execute. Let reality teach you. Reality is sharper and faster than any textbook. Studies are maps. Action is the territory.

You don't need another book, another podcast, or another class. You don't need permission from experts. You don't need a study to start. You need to move. Because the act of starting is the only authority that matters.

Chapter 52 — Start Small, End Ruthlessly

Mel Fisher spent 16 years chasing a dream most people would have abandoned in 16 weeks. The object of his obsession was the *Nuestra Señora de Atocha*, a Spanish galleon that sank off the Florida Keys in 1622 with a fortune of gold, silver, and emeralds aboard. Year after year, Fisher and his crew searched the ocean floor. They endured storms, financial ruin, endless dead ends, and even family tragedy. Most mornings they pulled up nothing but sand, shells, and scraps. And yet every morning, Fisher said the same words to his team before they dove again: "Today's the day."

That simple phrase was his way of shrinking the impossible into something manageable. He couldn't guarantee the year. He couldn't control the month. But he could start today. One more dive. One more search. One more step in the right direction. That's what a small start looks like.

And Fisher wasn't just good at starting. He was ruthless at ending. He cut false leads, ignored rumors, and shut down distractions. He refused to scatter his attention across a hundred possible wrecks. Every dive, every dollar, every ounce of energy went into the Atocha. Thousands of small starts, paired with thousands of ruthless endings, carried him forward.

In 1985—after 16 years—Fisher's crew finally struck gold. Literally. They discovered the wreck and pulled up over $400 million in treasure: gold bars, silver coins, chains, and emeralds. If you walk into the Mel Fisher Maritime Museum in Key West today, you can see the artifacts yourself. Coins, jewels, chalices, and bars of gold sit in glass cases. It's inspiring not just because of the wealth, but because of the method behind it. Treasure wasn't found through one grand beginning or one lucky ending. It was found through thousands of small starts and thousands of ruthless cuts.

That's the principle: start small, end ruthlessly.

Most people do the opposite. They try to start big—with ambitious timelines, elaborate plans, and massive goals. And they end soft, dragging things out, keeping dead weight alive, and refusing to cut losses. Big starts paralyze. Soft endings drain. Together, they kill momentum.

Small starts are powerful because they bypass resistance. A single rep. One email. One conversation. One dive. Something too small to resist, but real enough to move you forward. Big goals collapse under their own weight. Small starts compound.

Ruthless endings are powerful because they clear the field. Most people don't fail at beginning—they fail at closing. They hang on to projects that should be shut down. They pour time into distractions that should be cut. They keep going not because it's working, but because they've already invested. That's the sunk-cost fallacy: the human tendency to throw more resources into something just because you've already spent some. It's how companies bleed billions chasing failed products. It's how individuals waste years in jobs or relationships they know are wrong.

Fisher avoided the trap by cutting what didn't serve the mission. If a lead turned out false, he killed it. If a path proved empty, he ended it. His crew didn't dive everywhere hoping to get lucky. They focused, cut, and refocused. That discipline—ruthless endings—kept the search alive.

189

Psychology explains why this matters. The sunk-cost fallacy keeps people locked into losing bets. Ending ruthlessly breaks the chain and frees up energy. Parkinson's Law shows how work expands to fill the time allowed. Ruthless deadlines counter that by forcing closure. Pair the two together and you've got a sharp edge: you start so small you can't stall, and you end so hard you can't drift.

The power is in the cycle. Small starts create traction. Ruthless endings protect it. One without the other doesn't work. Start too big, you stall. End too soft, you suffocate. Start small, end ruthlessly—you build momentum that compounds without clutter.

Think about what Fisher's mantra meant: "Today's the day." He didn't say, "This year is the year." He didn't talk in decades. He didn't make the goal so big that it crushed the crew under its weight. He made it small enough to carry. Today. This dive. One shot. At the same time, he cut anything that didn't lead to the Atocha. That balance—small starts and ruthless endings— is why he succeeded where so many others gave up.

The museum in Key West isn't just a monument to treasure. It's a monument to method. Every gold bar and silver coin behind glass is a reminder of how small starts and ruthless endings build results that look impossible from the outside.

You don't need to be chasing shipwrecks to use the same principle. Any pursuit worth doing requires both. Shrink your beginnings until they're undeniable. Sharpen your endings until they're final. Protect the cycle. Repeat it daily. That's how treasure is found, books are written, systems are built, and lives are changed.

Start small. End ruthlessly.

Chapter 53 — From Rough Draft to Masterpiece

Every masterpiece begins as a mess. It's not an accident or a failure—it's the nature of creation, and more than that, the nature of starting. No sculptor begins with a statue; they begin with a block. No author starts with a bestseller, only a paragraph that barely holds together. Every entrepreneur you admire began with an idea that wobbled, a product that wasn't ready, or a plan that fell apart. What separated them was the nerve to begin—and to begin again—through every stage of that rough draft until it became something remarkable.

We forget how often the greats stumbled early. Hemingway rewrote the ending to *A Farewell to Arms* thirty-nine times. Van Gogh couldn't sell a single painting in his lifetime. Howard Schultz was turned down by investors who thought Americans didn't need a European-style coffeehouse. Walt Disney was once told he lacked imagination. Yet all of them had one thing in common: they started, and then they started again.

The rough draft isn't the shameful stage; it's the sacred one. It's proof that you're building something that didn't exist before, that you're willing to work through uncertainty instead of hiding behind perfection. It's not about lowering your standards—it's about separating the process from the product. You give yourself permission to iterate, to stay in the ring long enough to shape something worth showing. And when it stalls, you start again.

Look at Tom Brady in his early years—a sixth-round pick who treated every season like he still had to earn a roster spot. Jim Courier, who pioneered the power-baseline game and fought his way to World No. 1, wasn't handed anything; he rebuilt his game through sheer repetition and stubborn reinvention. And Diana Nyad, who failed again and again to swim from Cuba to Florida, came back in her sixties and finished what younger versions of herself couldn't. None of them saw the rough draft as beneath them. They understood it was the only way through. Each reset was a new start—and that's how mastery hardens.

The problem isn't imperfection; the problem is pretending you're past it. When you embrace the rough draft, you unlock momentum. You learn faster, recover faster, and discover what works by confronting what doesn't. That holds true in art, business, and relationships alike. If you wait for perfect, you'll wait forever. If you move forward while it's messy, progress happens.

Refinement can come later. The raw version has to exist first. No one gets to skip that stage, and no one who ever made it regrets it. Every overnight success is built on ten years of rough drafts you never saw. The best move you can make today is to ship version 1.0, share your half-formed idea, launch your imperfect product, and let the feedback hit. Let the fire shape it. Then rebuild and keep starting.

Rough drafts aren't failures; they're signals. They're seeds. Trust them—because that's how every masterpiece begins.

We've rewritten history to fit the myth. We treat geniuses as if they were born finished. But Beethoven wasn't divine inspiration in human form; he was obsession. He rewrote and edited his compositions relentlessly. Mozart, the so-called prodigy, was drilled by his father from the age of three and composed hundreds of works before fame ever found him. Leonardo da Vinci abandoned more paintings than he completed, filling pages with sketches, notes, and corrections.

192

Their greatness wasn't in their first strokes—it was in their refusal to settle.

Their brilliance came not from magic but from method. They practiced, corrected, destroyed, and rebuilt. They weren't magicians; they were relentless craftsmen. We weaken their legacy when we pretend it was easy. By turning the greats into myths, we give ourselves permission to stay small. We say, "I'm not gifted like them," instead of admitting, "I haven't worked like them." The truth is more empowering: if they forged their genius draft by draft, we can too. And if they started over again and again, so can we.

Genius isn't born complete; it's built. Greatness is a grind, each rough draft a new beginning. Behind every masterpiece are a thousand silent starts no one ever applauded. So start. Start rough. Start now.

What the greats discovered intuitively, science now confirms. Psychologist K. Anders Ericsson, whose work inspired the 10,000-hour rule, found that mastery isn't about time—it's about deliberate practice: focused effort just beyond your comfort zone, repeated with feedback and adjustment. That's starting, refined into a discipline. Later research by Josh Kaufman showed that major progress doesn't always take thousands of hours; around twenty hours of consistent, deliberate practice can move you from total beginner to competent. That's not genius—it's commitment multiplied by repetition.

So don't worship talent; practice starting. You don't need a decade or credentials. You need one deliberate beginning today, and another tomorrow. Whether it's writing, painting, coding, public speaking, or parenting, the first draft is enough to begin. The commitment to start again is what sharpens it. The rough draft is where skill is born, and the decision to restart is where it grows.

You're not one draft away; you're one start away—from discovering who you become through building, breaking, reshaping, and beginning again. Every masterpiece you admire is a pile of discarded drafts, late nights, awkward starts, and someone who refused to stop. Make your next start today—not to finish it all, but to begin it better than before.

That's the path. That's the truth. That's the power of starting rough—and starting again.

Chapter 54 — You Don't Owe Anyone the Final Version

Somewhere along the way, we were taught to wait until everything was figured out—to plan until the edges were smooth, to polish until we were proud, and only then release something into the world. That thinking kills momentum before it ever starts. You don't owe anyone the final version. You owe them honesty, movement, and a signal that you're alive and in it.

The first draft of your business, relationship, book, or life will be messy. Good. That means you're human. Growth doesn't happen inside perfection—it happens through iteration. The startup that launches a clunky beta gains real feedback. The writer who self-publishes learns what resonates. The coach who offers free sessions discovers what people value. Action reveals. Waiting hides.

We live in a culture obsessed with the highlight reel, where everything's filtered and curated. That illusion creates paralysis. People hold back because they don't want to look like they're trying. But starting means being seen trying. It means risking exposure. That's the price of creation—and the doorway to progress. You don't need approval; you need momentum. No one can argue with traction. Results earn their own respect. Don't delay your start waiting for a masterpiece. Let the work mature in public. Let your voice sharpen and your mission grow legs. But you have to begin.

We treat identity like it's something we declare after a ceremony. In truth, identity is shaped by motion. You don't become a runner when you get fast—you become one when you run. You don't become a builder when your project is perfect—you become one when you break ground. People respect real more than perfect. They lean in when they see movement, not polish. This doesn't mean be careless—it means be in motion. Improvement is the byproduct of commitment, not the prerequisite for it.

The final version is a myth. It's a moving target. If you wait for it, you'll never step forward. This is why so many viral videos aren't shot in studios—they're quick, raw iPhone clips. Real moments, real reactions. A dog slipping on ice. A kid saying something unexpected. A man breaking down in gratitude. These resonate because they're real. They're proof that people are drawn to authenticity more than perfection. In fact, research published in *Harvard Business Review* found that audiences perceive creators who show vulnerability as more trustworthy and engaging. The studio can come later. The polish can come later. But the moment must be captured now.

The "final" version is always just a snapshot—a comma, not a period. Every product, every piece of art, every self-reinvention is just the latest iteration. Tomorrow you'll see it clearer. Next week you'll do it better. So what? Today, you still build. That principle doesn't stop with business or art—it extends to how we live. I feel bad for the young couple who think they can't get married without a planner, a six-figure budget, and a production team. The sacred beginning gets swallowed by performance and debt. We've traded presence for presentation. The start is enough. The commitment is what matters, not the choreography.

Sara Blakely built Spa from an apartment floor with no fashion background, no final business plan, and no industry contacts.

She didn't wait to be qualified—she started. That single act turned into a billion-dollar brand, not because it launched perfectly, but because it launched at all. YouTube did the same. Its early uploads were grainy, glitchy, low-res. But they worked. Those imperfections invited participation. The same truth shows up in art: Bob Dylan's "Like a Rolling Stone" was recorded in one take—no polish, no redo—just raw conviction. The honesty of the performance made it immortal.

Too many people are rehearsing a life they never live—practicing a pitch they never give, revising a book they never publish, planning a business they never open. All because they believe the world deserves perfection first. It doesn't. The world deserves truth in motion. You don't owe perfection—you owe progress. Every moment spent waiting is a moment stolen from discovery, feedback, and growth.

Start ugly and start now. The world doesn't need your polished version someday; it needs your real, imperfect step today, with the rough edges showing and the work allowed to breathe, because that's the only version that ever gets better. You don't owe anyone the final version—you owe yourself the truth and the start.

PART VI — Starting Where it Matters

Chapter 55 — Start With the End in Mind

Most people never start because they never define what the finish looks like. They wander into a project, a business, a relationship, a routine—but they don't know what they're aiming at. And if you don't know the target, you'll either never fire, or worse, fire in every direction.

We've already talked about how culture worships the finish—trophies, titles, applause—and how that obsession kills the start. This chapter isn't about that. This isn't outcome worship. This is direction. There's a difference. A finish line you fantasize about will freeze you. A finish line you define—quietly, honestly—gives you a compass. One paralyzes. The other pulls you forward.

Starting with the end in mind isn't about obsessing over goals or chasing outcomes. It's about having a vision strong enough to keep you moving when the work gets rough. A vision is different from a fantasy. Fantasies live in comfort; vision lives in commitment. The athlete who envisions hoisting the trophy in the off-season, the father picturing his kids secure twenty years from now, the writer who already sees the book on the shelf—each is fueled by an image of completion vivid enough to pull them forward.

You don't need every step mapped, but you do need to feel the weight of where you're going. That sense of direction turns effort into momentum. Starting a diet? Know the kind of life you want to live around that body. Starting a company? Know the freedom or impact you're driving toward. Starting a relationship? Know the kind of love you intend to give, not just receive. When you skip that clarity, you start out of boredom or restlessness—and when it gets hard, you bail. No anchor, no finish line.

That's the real power of beginning with the end in mind: it gives you an internal compass when the map gets foggy. Stephen Covey named this decades ago, but many misunderstood it as scripting every step. It isn't control—it's clarity. It's saying, this is what matters, and shaping your effort around it.

Clarity is what filters distraction. When you know where you're going, you say no faster, waste less time, and endure more pressure because the end justifies the fire. Distractions aren't always obvious; sometimes they look like opportunity. They show up as side gigs that dilute focus, as endless research and planning, as scrolling disguised as learning, as chasing trends that drag you off mission. They feel productive—but they're not. Without an end in mind, they quietly steal your direction until you wake up miles from the finish you once envisioned.

The end in mind isn't rigid; it's alive. Ends evolve. They should. That evolution doesn't erase the original vision—it builds on it. Some of the greatest leaps in science, business, and art came from a clear initial goal that later expanded with new understanding. Psychologist Gabrielle Oettingen's research on "mental contrasting" found that pairing vivid visualization of a goal with awareness of real obstacles dramatically increases persistence. In other words, seeing the end clearly—even while knowing it will change—keeps you moving when willpower alone fades.

Consider the military. Its equipment standards were designed for survival under extreme conditions, not for consumer products. Yet those same principles—durability, reliability, precision—now shape industries from medicine to aerospace. The original end was simple: excellence under pressure. The application evolved, but the standard remained. That's what happens when intention runs deep.

Companies use mission statements for the same reason. The best ones don't hang them on a wall; they use them to steer real decisions. When the market shifts, they adapt the method but not the mission. You should do the same. Maybe you start a book and it becomes a podcast. Maybe your business for freedom turns into a platform for contribution. Maybe your marriage teaches giving instead of completion. Ends evolve, but they don't evaporate.

Starting with an end teaches discipline. It trains you to filter noise, to hold the line when the work feels dull, and to grow into a bigger vision. If you're launching something today—a habit, a hustle, or a hard conversation—zoom forward. Picture the finish in detail. How does it feel? Who benefits? What becomes possible because you finished? That image will fuel the start.

Even death reminds us of this principle. Every eulogy speaks of legacy—character, contribution, the love left behind—and that's the real end, so why not live that way now by reverse-engineering your daily starts from the end you'd be proud to claim. Start today with the end in mind and let that vision pull you when willpower runs dry, because not every path deserves your energy—only the ones that lead somewhere—and that's where your start belongs.

Chapter 56 — Start Again at the Headwaters

There's a reason people hike upstream. The headwaters are clean. Untouched. Alive. Something about starting where the current begins resets your soul.

We don't just need a change of pace—we need a change of origin. If life has gotten murky, complicated, or downstream from where you once began, there's only one thing to do: go back to the source. Start again at the headwaters.

This isn't regression. It's a return to clarity. To intention. To purity of effort.

After years in business, it's easy to forget why you started. You get swept by currents—profit, pressure, comparison. The thing you built starts to drift. The same happens in marriage, friendship, faith. One day you look up and realize: this isn't where I began. And it's not where I want to stay.

So go back. Not in time, but in spirit. Start again, upstream. Return to the quiet belief you had before anyone was watching. Before you were judged. Before the metrics mattered. Remember that early conviction—the one that felt almost embarrassing to say out loud. That's your headwaters.

Starting again doesn't mean erasing everything. It means reclaiming clean energy and cutting off what got contaminated along the way.

Consultants love to present neat models: introduction, growth, maturity, plateau, decline. Tidy. Predictable. Fatalistic. According to them, everything peaks, stagnates, and dies. But that's nonsense. It leaves no space for reinvention—no chapter for starting again. Apply that logic to your life, and you get a slow death disguised as stability.

Stagnation isn't fate. It's just friction. And friction can be overcome. Start again, and you stay alive.

That's how companies like Apple survived. Not by clinging to the original blueprint, but by returning to the source again and again—from computers to iPods, to iPhones, to services. Netflix followed the same current, flowing from DVD rentals to streaming, to production, to gaming.

Kodak, Blockbuster, BlackBerry—they stayed downstream. They refused the return. And they sank.

The same rule applies to individuals. Matthew McConaughey stepped out of typecast comfort and rebooted his career with dramatic roles. Andre Agassi rebuilt himself from burnout to Grand Slam champion. Katie Ledecky, the most dominant 800-meter and 1500-meter freestyle swimmer in history, has repeatedly re-engineered her stroke, training cycles, and race strategy to keep evolving at the top of her sport. Reinvention isn't luck. It's a habit of starting.

Yet the world rarely tells you to begin again. The message is: keep your head down, stay the course, don't rock the boat. But the boat's sinking. Few voices say: start fresh. Plant the seed. Return upstream. It won't look glamorous now, but it's the only thing that stays alive later.

The truth is, reinvention is the antidote to decay. Starting again keeps your spirit young. Sometimes it means shutting down a product line that doesn't reflect your values. Sometimes it's rewriting a morning routine, reaching out to someone you drifted from, or deleting half your calendar so you can breathe again.

Even success needs renewal. Coasting feels safe—but it's a quiet form of decline. Stability isn't always strength; sometimes it's stagnation in disguise.

Ask yourself: Am I still building? Still learning? Still challenging myself? If not, maybe you need a new beginning—not from scratch, but from a truer place.

Neuroscientist Richard Davidson found that deliberate change activates neural plasticity—the brain's ability to rewire and grow at any age. That's what starting again really is: rewiring your direction to match your truth.

This chapter isn't a technique; it's a challenge. Go find your source and don't just look at it—drink from it, starting again not downstream or halfway through, but at the headwaters where your momentum is clean, the current still listens, and your direction isn't borrowed. That's where truth still flows, where the most powerful way forward begins, and where your next start is waiting if you're willing to walk back, get clear, and begin again.

Chapter 57 — What you Start Shapes You

You are what you do consistently—but even more than that, you are what you begin. Starts leave marks. They leave a pattern, a tilt, a pull. The business you launch, the tone you set in a new relationship, the first habits you pick when trying to rebuild your life—all of it becomes a blueprint that shapes who you become long after the thrill of the start fades. We like to imagine we're endlessly flexible, that identity is something we can easily reassign later. But the truth is sharper: who you become grows out of how you begin.

Start a business built on discounting and you will train customers to see you as cheap. Start a fitness routine with shortcuts and excuses and you will condition yourself for softness. Start your mornings with chaos, screens, and reactivity and you will wire your mind to chase noise instead of meaning. These aren't isolated events—they are identity scripts. The beginning writes the code you will eventually live inside.

Psychology has a name for this: the primacy effect. The earliest actions—those first few steps—carry more weight than anything that follows. We form impressions of people within three seconds. Investors decide whether to trust a founder within the first two minutes of a pitch. Teachers can predict academic engagement from the opening week of a semester. The beginning doesn't just matter—it imprints.

In your own life, this imprint shapes how you move. Start with generosity and your instinct becomes to give. Start with order and you become someone who values clarity. Start with fear and you internalize hesitation. Start with courage and even your doubts eventually learn to follow you into battle. We don't simply form habits; habits quietly form us.

Elite performers understand this intuitively. They don't waste energy polishing the end. They perfect the entrance. Sprinters rehearse their stance in the blocks because they know that one twitch in the opening half-second can cost the entire race. Golfers obsess over the takeaway because the swing is decided in the first inch. Speakers rehearse their first sentence more than their last. Musicians drill the opening bars until they can play them half asleep. Actors anchor their presence in the first breath they take on stage. They understand that beginnings are leverage points. Once the start is clean, the rest follows a stronger line.

The same is true outside performance. A relationship shaped by avoidance on day one evolves into a relationship defined by silence years later. A company birthed through chaos becomes a company that runs on crisis management. A financial life built on impulse hardens into a life built on regret. Starts don't just predict outcomes—they construct them.

This doesn't mean you need dramatic openings. It means you need intentional ones. When you begin something new—your health, your work, your craft, your money, your commitments—treat the start with respect. The first tone you set becomes the default tone later. Most regrets people carry aren't from catastrophic mistakes; they're from casual beginnings. They drifted into patterns that quietly rewrote who they were.

Think about your life right now. Think about the places where beginnings matter: the first thing you do each morning, the way you open your workday, the way you reconnect with your partner after distance, the way you treat money on payday, the way you enter the gym, the way you pick up the pen, the way you walk into silence when you pray or think or reset. These aren't small moves. They're identity-setting rituals. Each start is a vote for the type of person you're becoming.

The irony is that sloppy starts usually happen because people underestimate them. They assume they can fix the tone later. But later rarely comes. Once the pattern sets, you don't rise above it—you repeat it. The start becomes the mold.

But here's the good news: starts are renewable. You can start again with more intention any time you choose. You can rewrite the opening line of any chapter of your life—health, career, love, purpose, faith. You can return to clarity and reset the tone. This isn't reinvention; it's a return to authorship.

Every meaningful change in life begins with a deliberate start. And that start doesn't have to be dramatic. It just has to be clean. A clean start creates momentum. A clean start reshapes narrative. A clean start builds identity that can hold under pressure.

What you start shapes you. Start with intention. Start with clarity. Start like the beginning matters—because it does. And if you've begun poorly, start again. The opening moment is never lost. It's always waiting to be rewritten by the next start you choose.

Chapter 58 — The Start is the Seed

You've been lied to about time.
They told you to manage it, track it, color-code it, even weaponize it. But time doesn't care about your lists or planners. It doesn't reward intentions. Time follows the start. Nothing in your day matters until the start happens. Once it does, time bends. Minutes stretch. Hours clarify. Momentum appears. The fog lifts. Your mind stops negotiating, and your body begins to move.

The start is the seed. Everything else is just dirt until you plant it.

Most people chase an illusion. They think controlling time means controlling output. But that's backward. You don't manage time—you activate it. You unlock it. And the only honest way to unlock it is by starting. That's why so many people end their days feeling like they did nothing. The calendar was full, the list was long, but the seed was never planted. They circled the work, prepped, planned, thought— but never began. Planning without starting is procrastination in disguise.

Traditional productivity advice misses this. It glorifies control and underestimates courage. It treats time as a container instead of a current. It tricks you into believing that scheduling a task equals progress. But only one act grows something from nothing: the start.

Goals suffer the same flaw. A goal without motion is a wish with a deadline. Motion only begins with a first move. Starting turns the abstract into the actual. Think of all the goals you've written that never lived—not because they were bad goals, but because the start never came. A seed that isn't planted doesn't fail; it just never becomes. If goals are the fruit, starting is the seed—and too many people fantasize about harvest without touching soil.

You don't need more goals. You need more starts.

Your day isn't a machine to optimize; it's a field to cultivate. The first thing you plant shapes everything that follows. The first task of the day has disproportionate power—it sets the frame, flips the brain from indecision to movement. Delay the start, and the day grows sideways. But plant one good start early, even a small one, and you tilt the whole field toward harvest.

Start small. Start early. Plant one thing that matters. Everything else will grow around it.

Forget time blocks. What you need are start blocks—short bursts devoted purely to ignition. No pressure to finish. Just permission to begin. A start block can be ten minutes or three. The power isn't in duration; it's in ignition. Once you move, you'll often keep moving. But even if you don't, you've shifted the energy. You've told the day who's in charge.

Time doesn't respond to pressure. It responds to clarity. And starting gives it clarity.

You don't reclaim time by wishing for it. You reclaim it by moving. Every start rescues a fragment of your day—a sliver of energy, purpose, and strength. A good start doesn't just produce work; it rewires identity. It reminds you that you're a person of action, not someone stuck in reaction. That's why starting feels uncomfortable—it confronts the lie that you have no control. But once you move, even for sixty seconds, control returns.

Every real start is a rescue mission. You're pulling yourself from the quicksand of hesitation and setting your feet on solid ground. That's not small. That's holy.

Some people stay stuck because they overthink the start. They want the perfect seed, the right order, the flawless plan. But seeds don't need to be perfect. They just need to be planted.

If you're unsure where to begin, choose something that matters—even a little. Something you can touch in ten minutes. Something that stirs you emotionally, spiritually, or creatively. It doesn't have to be big. Just real. A phone call. A paragraph. A sketch. A walk. A prayer. A pitch. One planted seed can tilt your entire world toward motion. One Start Signal can clear a day's worth of fog.

You already carry a natural timing system inside you. You feel it when energy rises after movement, when one start leads to another. That's not coincidence; it's biology. Behavioral science calls it activation energy—once you begin, dopamine follows, not before. Your body is wired to reward motion. You just have to stop overriding it with guilt, distraction, and digital noise.

Let that go. Build your day around what your body already knows: start first, and the rest follows.

This truth shows up everywhere—across systems far bigger than you. The most complex man-made procedures on earth aren't midstream operations; they're starts. Nuclear power plants, refineries, rocket engines, massive turbines—these systems require specialized startup engineers whose entire expertise is the first ignition. Not the maintenance. Not the shutdown. The start. Because the start determines stability. Once a plant is successfully brought online, it can run smoothly for twenty years. But none of that reliability exists until the first ignition holds. The entire lifespan of the system hinges on the quality of the beginning. These people are responsible for waking up megastructures.

They bring giants online. And they treat the start with a level of respect bordering on reverence.

That's your job too — not with steel and turbines, but with your life.

The economy works the same way. Startup entrepreneurs—real builders—are the lifeblood of culture. They create jobs, industries, breakthroughs. Nations compete for them. Investors chase them. Entire ecosystems form around the person willing to start something from nothing. And the same principle applies to your life. You are the startup engineer of your own direction. If the beginning is clean, the rest can run for years off its momentum.

People overcomplicate progress. They chase hacks, tricks, and frameworks. But at the end of the day, it's the same truth every high-performer discovers: it's the start, stupid.

Even the famous "make your bed" advice—often repeated, often misunderstood—was never about bedsheets. The power wasn't the task; it was the ignition. The ritual of beginning the day with a deliberate action. That was the real message hiding underneath the simplicity. The same goes for the person who starts the morning with ten push-ups, a short prayer, or a two-minute journal entry. It doesn't matter what the act is. It matters that it's an act. A seed planted. A signal sent.

AA has known this for a century. Their motto—"one day at a time"—is really a philosophy of daily beginnings. The first thing many recovering addicts do each morning is drop to their knees and ask their higher power for guidance. Not because the gesture fixes everything, but because it *starts* everything. Each day is treated as a new ignition cycle. A new seed. A new start. And it works.

Even Genesis follows this structure. Creation wasn't one explosion of perfection; it was a series of starts—day after day after day. Light. Land. Life. Order. Each morning was a new beginning. The blueprint for existence begins with a start.

That seed you're afraid to plant holds everything—not just the task, but your integrity, your identity, your fire. It holds your peace, your power, your breakthrough. Every excuse—too tired, too late, too uncertain—only exists because the seed isn't planted yet. Start, and the excuse disappears. Start, and time unlocks. Start, and the goal becomes real. The seed isn't the beginning of the work. It is the work. Once it's planted, everything else becomes response.

Don't wait for clarity, the perfect plan, or until you "have time." You already have the seed—use it, because the start isn't just part of the journey; it is the seed, and the seed holds everything.

Chapter 59 — The World Doesn't Reward You for Waiting

We're taught to wait. Wait your turn. Wait for the right moment. Wait until you're ready. But the world doesn't reward waiting. It rewards movement.

The people who wait for clarity miss the window. The ones who wait for perfect timing never get started. The ones who wait to be picked get passed over by those who choose themselves. Who gets ahead? The starters. The movers. The ones who act while others hesitate. They're not always the smartest or most gifted—but they're in motion. Motion beats perfection. Action beats ideas. Momentum beats fear.

You can prepare forever and still get flattened the first time life hits back. Starting is better than waiting because starting teaches what waiting never will. Waiting teaches hesitation. Starting teaches grit. Every breakthrough in your life will come after motion—never before. The job, the client, the deal, the insight, the change—none of them appear in the waiting room. They show up on the trail, in the middle of the mess, when your hands are already dirty.

We romanticize readiness, as if someday all the lights will turn green and the wind will be at our backs. But that day never comes. Life doesn't roll out a red carpet. You roll up your sleeves. You don't need perfect timing. You need a pulse. You need presence. You need to trust that forward motion, even if wobbly, opens more doors than standing still ever will. Psychologists call this the action bias: when faced with uncertainty, successful people default to doing something while others freeze. That instinct—to move rather than wait—is what separates momentum from stagnation.

Think about the people you admire. Are they the ones who waited? Or the ones who moved? Most likely, they were the ones who took a step before it made sense, who risked looking foolish, who started before they were ready. The most powerful starts in the world often go unnoticed. Someone wakes up early. Sends the email. Signs up for the class. These acts seem small, but they shift trajectories. They plant the seed that waiting never will.

You don't have to sprint. You don't have to explode out of the gate. But you have to move. Waiting doesn't build the muscle. Motion does. Like training, the first reps are the hardest—but they make everything else possible. Too many people waste years waiting for a green light. The truth is simple: the world is full of yellow lights. Mixed signals. Unclear paths. If you're waiting for a perfect sign, you'll wait forever.

You don't need permission to start a business, to write the book, to rebuild a relationship, or to finally speak up. You only need a pulse and a small dose of courage. I've watched brilliant people wait their entire lives—for more confidence, more proof, more validation—and they missed it. Because the world doesn't hand you guarantees. It hands you chances. And chances are only useful to those who move.

Starting transforms you. It gives you feedback, sharpens your instincts, and turns you from a thinker into a doer. You don't become who you're meant to be by standing still. Even the wrong start is better than none—because once you're moving, you can steer. But you can't steer a parked car.

Let's be honest: waiting is usually fear in disguise. Fear of failure. Fear of looking foolish. Fear of wasting time. But the irony is brutal—waiting is the real waste. One week of motion can change more than a year of overthinking. One conversation can shift a relationship. One act of courage can rewrite your story.

You want results, progress, meaning? Then don't wait—start before the conditions are perfect, before confidence shows up, while you're unsure, unqualified, and underestimated, because the world doesn't reward waiting, it rewards movement. Start now, start messy, start anyway, and do it while everyone else is still waiting.

Chapter 60 — Start the Prayer, Not the Plan

Most people start with a plan. We map it out, list the goals, line up the steps, create timelines. Then we try to muscle through with grit. Sometimes it works—but more often, it burns us out. Starting with a plan without centering it in prayer is like building a house on sand. You might get the walls up fast, but you'll feel the cracks when the pressure hits.

The better way? Start the prayer. Start the stillness. Start the conversation with God—the One who sees the whole board. Begin from a posture that says, I don't have to figure it all out right now. I just have to ask, listen, and move from peace. Prayer isn't about sounding holy. It's not about pretending to be calm. It's about alignment—about starting from the core instead of the chaos. You want clarity? Start the prayer. You want courage? Start the prayer. You want peace in the process, not just pride in the outcome? Start the prayer.

Plans are useful, but they're reactive. Prayer is proactive. It changes how you see, not just what you do. Too many people treat prayer like a break from progress. It's not. It's the source of it—the place where real direction lives. Prayer says, I don't want to just get things done. I want to get the right things done.

You don't need a perfect routine. You need a consistent return—a way to ground yourself every day before the noise begins. Before every mission, a fighter pilot runs a pre-flight checklist. Not because they forgot how to fly, but because the stakes are too high to rely on memory alone. Prayer is your spiritual pre-flight. It's not delay—it's preparation. Quiet, focused, essential.

And it doesn't have to be long. Sometimes the shortest prayer—"Help me." "Guide me." "Speak, I'm listening."—opens more doors than a week of strategy sessions. Start the prayer before the pitch, before the launch, before the meeting or the call. Let your mind get quiet enough to receive, not just react.

This isn't about religion. It's about rhythm. It's not about being spiritual. It's about being sane. Studies even show that prayer and meditation lower cortisol, quiet the default-mode network in the brain, and heighten focus—the physiological proof that peace precedes power. Prayer doesn't shrink ambition; it centers it. It doesn't dull your drive; it clarifies it.

The greatest work you'll ever do won't come from control—it'll come from surrender. From the simple posture that says, Use me. Start the prayer, not the plan. Let the rest follow.

Look at anyone who rebuilt their life, changed their direction, or rose from a place they thought they'd never escape. Their turning point wasn't a perfect plan. It was a moment of humility. A moment of surrender. A moment when they finally said, God, take the lead. The human heart needs anchoring before it needs instruction. And prayer is that anchor.

If it works at the hardest moments of a person's life, it can work before the pressure, before the push, before the plan—and when you forget, you start again. Before you keep reading this book, stop for one breath, one whisper, one line to God, because that's the kind of start that changes everything.

Chapter 61 — Marriage Begins Again Every Day

Marriage isn't a ceremony. It isn't the photo album or the rings or the anniversary posts. Marriage is what happens after all of that—and it either decays slowly in the background of your life or it begins again every single day. You don't renew your vows every ten years. You renew them every morning by how you show up. You choose again. Not in grand gestures, but in the quiet decision to give, to listen, to stay present, to hold the line when it would be easier to let go. Marriage is a discipline of starting.

You start again after a fight. You start again when the feelings fade. You start again when you feel unseen, tired, stressed, or overworked. You start again even when the other person doesn't notice. And that's the secret: love that lasts is built on starts that don't stop. The biggest threats to marriage aren't always betrayal or financial strain. More often, they're drift, disconnection, and silence. The way you fight them isn't with books or trips—it's by choosing to start again before you feel like it.

Start the touch. Start the conversation. Start the forgiveness. Start the humor. Start the grace. Marriage doesn't thrive on ease. It thrives on intention. That's why so many couples who once fell in love end up living like roommates—they stopped starting. They coasted. They waited for the other person to go first. But real strength in a relationship isn't about who's right. It's about who's willing. Willing to start the repair. Willing to give before they get. Willing to build even when it's slow and messy.

You want to know the cost of not starting? Distance. Resentment. Lost years. The couples you admire—the ones who still laugh together after thirty years—didn't get lucky. They just never stopped starting. They made the first move. They bit their tongue. They said yes to the ordinary. They forgave loudly and celebrated quietly. They didn't keep score. They just kept moving.

Marriage is less about being in love and more about staying in motion. And motion requires a start. Even when you're annoyed. Even when they're distant. Especially then. Start the kind word. Start the touch. Start the prayer. Start the meal. Start the walk. And yes, you'll have to start again tomorrow. That's not a burden. That's the beauty. It's proof you're still in it.

Marriage begins again every day—and the couples who remember that are the ones who last. They don't wait for love to feel easy. They start anyway. I don't claim to be an expert. No one is. The moment you think you've figured marriage out, life humbles you. There are hundreds of ways to make it work—and just as many ways to drift apart. But this truth holds: the moment you stop starting, things start slipping. And the moment you begin again, even in the smallest way, something reopens.

Relationship researcher John Gottman calls these small moments "bids for connection"—tiny gestures of reaching out, looking, touching, asking. His studies show that couples who respond to these bids positively more than 80% of the time stay together decades longer. Why? Because they keep starting.

I've felt this in my own marriage. After a disagreement or a miscommunication, when the air feels tight and the silence starts growing roots, I used to make the mistake of trying to untangle everything—rehash the details, explain what I meant, clarify every point. It never helped. It usually made things worse. What finally worked was something simpler. I'd look at my wife and say, "Honey, can we restart everything? I don't know what happened, but can we restart? I'm sorry." And that reset—without a lecture, without a post-mortem—fixed more than any explanation ever did. Sometimes the restart is the repair.

Sometimes I think about how even animals model this truth. Two dogs can get into a brutal fight—snarling, snapping, teeth bared—and after a pause, you bring them back together and the energy shifts. They sniff, they circle, but the fight is gone. The pause reset something primal. No words, no apologies— just a new start.

Humans don't reset as easily. We hold grudges longer. But we also have something animals don't: choice. The ability to look at the person we love after a hard day, a stupid argument, or a long silence and decide: I'm starting again. And that choice— that quiet, inner restart—is what marriage is made of.

Chapter 62 — The Power of Starting With Your Kids

No one gets a cleaner slate than a child. Every morning, they wake up new. And the hardest part of parenting—especially for those wired for performance, goals, or control—is slowing down long enough to meet them there. At the start. That's where the power is: starting with your kids. Not correcting. Not preaching. Not pushing. Starting—with presence, with curiosity, with a willingness to connect before you control.

Most parents lead with the end in mind. They want the discipline, the grades, the college acceptance, the career, the checklist. But starting with your kids means letting go of the outcome—at least for a moment—and joining them in the beginning. You kneel beside them in the mess. You ask better questions. You look them in the eye. You start again after a bad day. You apologize. You become the kind of parent who says, We start here—not because you deserve it, but because you're worth it.

Start with a smile. Start with a question. Start with your phone down. Start when they least expect it—not with a lecture, but with love. Because kids don't always remember what you said. They remember how you began. Were you cold? Were you short? Did you rush, or did you slow down enough to see what they were feeling before you reacted? That start builds the emotional tone of the relationship. And the beautiful thing is— you get to start again every day. You can change the pattern with one decision: This morning, I start with love.

Here's the deeper truth: the start they experience with you

becomes the start they learn to give themselves. When you meet them with curiosity instead of shame, they learn to ask better questions inside their own mind. When you let them fail without condemning them, they learn how to recover without self-hate. Starting with your kids isn't about letting them off the hook. It's about giving them a stronger one—a way of thinking that isn't ruled by fear or performance. Some kids are easy. Some test every ounce of patience you have. But the start isn't about them. It's about you. About leading the emotional tone with stability and grace—especially when they have none.

When you start with love, you give them a frame that echoes in their head for decades. My dad didn't blow up. My mom actually listened. They showed up. That's what sticks. Psychologist Daniel Siegel calls this "emotional attunement"— the moment a child feels seen, safe, soothed, and secure. It's not about perfect parenting; it's about consistent reconnection. We talk a lot about generational wealth. But generational emotional wealth—that's what you're building. And it starts with the start.

Start the conversation. Start the apology. Start the laugh. Start the morning. Start the repair. Start the tradition. Not when it's easy, but when it's needed most. You will never regret starting. You will regret waiting. Kids grow fast. What people really mean when they say that is: you won't always get another chance to start. So take the ones you have now.

And don't confuse loving your kids with loving being a parent. They're not the same. Loving your kids is quiet, relentless, inconvenient. It shows up when you're tired, when they're ungrateful, when you'd rather check out. That kind of love is a discipline. A start. Every time you lean in when you want to walk out, you're giving them a deeper root. Every time you forgive before they ask, you're teaching them grace. Every time you start with calm instead of chaos, you're regulating their nervous system and anchoring their world. That's leadership.

You don't need the perfect plan. You just need to make the next start the right one. Start with the hug. Start with the walk. Start with the truth. Start with the breakfast. Start with the do-over. That's the power of starting with your kids. It doesn't take perfection—just one intentional step, repeated often enough to become who they are. And who you are too.

Because the goal isn't to raise perfect kids—it's to raise kids who know how to start again. Children aren't a distraction from your mission. They're your greatest mission. The wealth that doesn't fit in a spreadsheet. We want to win in public without losing at home. To build brands, income, and legacy—but not at the cost of what truly matters.

If I can anchor this one truth—of starting, of presence, of leadership—with your kids, then this book has done its job. Because transformation without love is noise. And impact without home is hollow. Start with your kids. That's where real legacy lives. And if you're wired for ROI, here it is: the return on presence is trust. The return on patience is connection. The return on starting well is a child who knows they are loved, even when they fail. That's the only return that compounds forever.

Chapter 63 — Start With Love, Even When It's Hard

Starting with love sounds nice—until you're asked to prove it. Until you're in the room with someone who betrayed you. Until you're swallowed by rejection, dismissal, or silence. That's when the idea stops being poetic and becomes a test. Even then, you choose: start with love, stand with strength.

Love in relationships isn't soft. It's strong. Strong enough to tell the truth without cruelty. Strong enough to show up when walking away feels safer. Starting with anger is easy. Starting with love—that's discipline. That's clarity. It wins not because it feels good, but because it works.

Most people flinch at hurt. They bottle it, blow up, or break. They start with defense—or worse, revenge. But the loudest person is rarely the one who won. The one who starts with love, even in pain, already has ground beneath their feet. Because love isn't surrender—it's power under control. It's a boundary honored and a heart still open.

You start with love, not for them—but for you. So you don't carry poison. So you don't rehearse grievance forever. So you can move forward without dragging the weight of bitterness behind you.

The same is true for work. You love what you do—until it hurts. Every creator hits that wall. You pour in your best, only to be ignored, criticized, or dismissed. But you start with love anyway. Love for the craft. Love for the process. Love because it built you more than it broke you. You choose again: press record, open the document, paint the day. That's love at work. It demands grit. It means showing up, even while bleeding. It's the courage to push through until the work begins to push back.

J. Paul Getty once said: "Build wealth as a by-product of your business success. If wealth is your only objective, you will probably fail." He didn't chase money. He chased mastery. He loved figuring things out—the markets, the leverage, the puzzle itself. Rule #6 in his guide to success: wealth is the benefit, not the goal. That's what starting with love looks like in business. It isn't emotional—it's strategic. Getty's love hurt him. It cost him sleep, relationships, even peace. But he kept starting. Because love for the process always demands risk. And risk is how impact begins.

In relationships, love looks like showing up, speaking truth, being vulnerable—not in grand gestures, but in steady courage. In your work, love looks like creating through rejection, producing through silence, and staying in motion when others stop. Love isn't about chasing dopamine. It's about choosing discipline.

True wealth—the kind that compounds quietly—comes from that love. It's not loud. It's invisible at first. It grows from contribution, not applause. When you help, improve, or create—even when nobody's watching—you shift the world's balance toward value. That's what the invisible hand really means.

Start with love. Not because it makes sense. Because it works.

I once knew a Jesuit priest—Father Llorente—who lived this

principle in full. His love for the faith wasn't sentimental; it was examined and strong. He used to say, almost defiantly, "It makes sense." He meant that love—especially God's love—wasn't blind emotion but logic made flesh. His faith cost him comfort and popularity, but he started with love anyway. That kind of conviction doesn't make you fragile. It makes you immovable.

Sometimes, when the grind feels heavy and the praise is scarce, pause and ask: Am I loving this? Not romantically—strategically. Love the seed, not just the harvest. Love the soil, even when it's mud. Love the sun and the rain, even when they come at the wrong time. Most people only love the full-grown plant, but anyone worth listening to knows: real love begins when the thing is still small, fragile, maybe invisible.

If you only love the reward, you'll quit during the process. If you only love applause, you'll never learn to build in silence. But if you love the work—even when it hurts—you won't just survive. You'll evolve. Neuroscientists call this affective resilience: the ability to transform stress into growth through meaning and purpose. Love does that. It literally re-centers your brain and restores strength where stress would otherwise consume it.

In 1971, Bill Backer—creative director at McCann-Erickson—was stranded in an Irish airport café. Flights were grounded. Tempers flared. Then something shifted. Strangers began talking, laughing, sharing bottles of Coke. That moment sparked one of the most iconic campaigns in history: "I'd Like to Buy the World a Coke." Backer later wrote that ideas are like newborns—fragile, defenseless, easily crushed by data and committee. He said the biggest threat to a good idea isn't failure—it's premature exposure. That's love in action:

protecting what's small until it can stand.

Your work deserves that same love—guard it, feed it, keep it close in its early days when it can't defend itself, because if you don't love it when it's small, you'll never get to love it when it's big. So start with love, especially when it's fragile, especially when it hurts, especially when others tell you to quit, because that's when love matters most.

Chapter 64 — The Start That Heals the Family

Sometimes the start isn't just for you. Sometimes the thing you begin—the repair, the outreach, the apology, the habit, the tone—becomes the spark that shifts a whole household. We forget how contagious action is. Especially in families. Especially in the silence between people who live together but have stopped showing up for each other. We wait for the other person to change. We loop. We stall. We blame. We stew. All while the weight thickens.

But motion breaks it. One decision to act—without waiting to feel ready, without waiting to be right—can reroute the emotional current of a home. Start the walk. Start the meal. Start the cleanup. Start the conversation. Start the thing you think shouldn't be your job. Because maybe it is. Maybe it always was. Maybe you go first—not because they deserve it, but because the momentum needs a spark, and you're the one who can give it.

When a family system is stuck, someone has to break the inertia. That's the work of leadership. And leadership isn't a title—it's initiative. Whoever goes first leads. Not every start will fix everything, but every start can shift the tone. And sometimes that's all you need—a crack in the ice, a breach in the loop.

One of my favorite lines in a disagreement is, "Can we start over again?" Tempers may have flared. Someone may have been wronged. But that question softens everything. It cuts through pride. Most people are fine with a reset—because deep down, most people want peace more than they want to win. "Can we start over?" doesn't erase tension, but it disarms it. It invites humility without demanding an apology. It brings everyone back to the present.

Don't wait for unity to act. Act to build unity. I call it everyday starter leadership. Not the buzzword kind plastered across books. Not the abstract role of "visionary" or "chief delegator." Real leadership isn't posture—it's motion. It's doing what needs to be done, whether or not anyone notices. True leaders don't announce themselves. They just move. They pick up the pieces. They start the repair. They move toward the problem.

There are homes filled with resentment and silence that could shift overnight with one simple act. Not a speech. Not a confrontation. Just a start. One person willing to make dinner. One willing to ask a question without sarcasm. One willing to say, "Want to take a walk?" That's what love does—it moves before it calculates.

When in doubt, start with love. Start with what heals. It's not weakness to go first. It's strength. It's not losing to start the repair. It's leadership—taking action without needing permission or applause. Start where the cycle has been stuck the longest.

Behavioral research shows that only about ten percent of people are what psychologists call initiators—those wired to act without waiting for consensus, clarity, or validation. The rest tend to mirror the group or delay. Some of that is inherited. Some is learned. If you were raised in a home where no one apologized first, forgave first, or started first, then breaking that inertia may feel unnatural. But it's not permanent.

You can rewrite it. You can become the one who moves. The one who begins. The one who models. You can break the cycle by breaking the silence, by breaking the loop, by breaking the habit of waiting. That's not just healing the moment. That's healing a lineage.

You want to raise kids who lead? Show them how to start. Let them watch you go first—not with lectures, but with movement. Let them see everyday starter leadership in action. That's the deeper work. The pattern interrupt that resets the tone not just for today, but for generations.

I once heard about a man who hadn't spoken to his father in over twenty years. The reason? A fight over a baseball cap. It started when his uncle insulted him, and the father said nothing. No defense. No follow-up. Just silence. And that silence hardened into decades. It sounds ridiculous—a hat? But humans get stuck easier than we admit. Small slights become deep wounds when no one moves. And the longer you wait, the heavier the movement feels.

But that loop could have been broken with a single start—a phone call, a text, a visit, a simple, honest line like "Can we start over again?"—because that's all it takes to interrupt decades of pride. People don't need dramatic reconciliation; they need a crack in the armor, a signal that it's safe to come back to the table, and that signal rarely arrives on its own. Someone has to send it, and that someone can be you, because every family waiting for healing is really waiting for one person to start.

Chapter 65 — Break the Loop Fast

You already know the loop. It goes like this: you hesitate, you wait, you check your phone, you rethink your plan, you rearrange your to-do list, you feel guilty, you open a new tab, you scroll, you distract yourself, you promise to start in ten minutes. Then ten becomes thirty, and the window closes. That's the loop. And the only way out is fast. Hesitation compounds. Every second you stall makes the task heavier, the energy weaker, the excuses louder. Your brain starts layering on meaning: I don't feel ready. This must not be the right time. Maybe I need more research. I should probably clean my workspace first. False. You don't need more prep—you need to interrupt the loop.

Breaking the loop isn't about brute force. It's about speed—action before analysis, movement before mood. The only antidote to the mental spiral is something physical, immediately. Don't negotiate with it or try to build momentum inside the loop. You break it like you'd break glass: quick and total. Stand up, walk, pick up the pen, open the call, send the draft, start the thing. Whatever that first action is, take it without ceremony or readiness, without your coffee being perfect or your mood being right. The moment you act, the loop breaks. With it, all the tension and delay collapse, and you regain access to your real energy.

You don't need to feel good to start—you need to start to feel good. The first action is the gateway. Once you touch the project, the paper, the canvas, the call—the resistance dies. Not fully, not forever, but enough to shift you back into reality. Most people lose whole days waiting for the loop to break itself. It won't. It strengthens the longer it runs, feeding on hesitation. Its single purpose is to preserve stasis—to keep you mentally engaged and physically still.

So do the opposite. Start physically. You don't need rituals, power poses, or soundtracks. Just move. Tony Robbins is right that physiology shapes psychology, but you don't need a seminar to prove it. The body leads; the mind follows. A University of Wisconsin study found that lab rats trapped in a repetitive reward-delay pattern only broke it when given a forced physical nudge. The motion—not the thought—reset their behavior. Humans are no different. We don't think our way out of hesitation; we move our way out.

Even ancient institutions understood the power of an interruption. The Catholic Church built an entire ritual around it: the sacrament of penance. Strip away the theology and look at the structure—it's a reset mechanism. A formal break in the loop. Confession isn't just about moral bookkeeping; it's a psychological clean page. A sanctioned moment to stop the old pattern, acknowledge it, and begin again. That's why the Church recommends it not yearly or occasionally, but regularly—monthly, even weekly. They understood something behavioral scientists only named recently: people need structured resets. They need a moment where the loop is paused and a new start becomes possible. You don't have to be religious to understand the psychology. Every life needs interruption points. Every habit cycle needs a place where you can cut the script and begin again.

There are careers where looping doesn't hurt—bureaucratic jobs, administrative chains, meetings that pay you for waiting. The system absorbs delay and rewards the illusion of motion. But in high-agency work—sales, art, entrepreneurship, writing, building anything new—the loop kills. Delay equals death. The window closes while you're refreshing your feed. In those arenas, the only advantage you have is starting faster than the loop can grip you.

Children are natural loop-breakers. They don't analyze their emotional state or wait for perfect conditions. If they want to build, they grab blocks. If they want to run, they run. If they fall, they try again. Their instinct is direct: see something— engage it. Adults lose that reflex somewhere along the way. We overdevelop the thinking brain and underuse the doing body. We trade curiosity for caution and call it maturity. But that child instinct isn't gone—it's just buried. And the fastest way to uncover it isn't therapy or a vision board. It's motion. The same rule applies: see something—engage it.

Break the loop fast, hard, without emotion or hesitation. The magic of starting only works if you interrupt the stall before it becomes identity. One move, one touch, one trigger—that's all it takes. Then the next, and the next. You're back in control. Break the loop fast. Start anyway.

Chapter 66 — Wealth Begins With a Small Start

Wealth doesn't arrive all at once. It creeps. It collects. It compounds quietly long before anyone sees it. Most people miss it because they're chasing explosions—the six-figure day, the million-dollar flip, the viral win. But true wealth, the kind that frees you and endures, begins smaller. It's built in quiet corners, through habits that look insignificant until time reveals their force.

Everyone wants the windfall, but the better path is motion. Not a lottery ticket. Not a big swing. Just a start. A single product. A single skill. A single habit. It won't feel rich—it'll feel ridiculous. But that small beginning, repeated long enough, becomes what others later call luck. By the time they notice, the invisible work is already done.

That's the part no one teaches: wealth creeps up on you. It's not just built by intention, but by invisible forces you trigger the moment you start. Adam Smith called it the "invisible hand"—not only an economic idea but a truth about life. Every time you create something useful, you set value in motion. The system multiplies it, and through that movement, you gain too—not by extraction, but by exchange.

The irony is that the fastest way to build wealth is to stop chasing money. Focus on solving something. Shipping something. Contributing something. Each small act of value creation, especially the ones that seem too small to matter, tilts the odds in your favor. The invisible hand only moves when your hands move first.

Start the blog. Record the video. Build the prototype. Contact the manufacturer. Print five shirts. Launch a three-day ebook. Offer to help. Trade a favor. Post the photo. Give away what you know. None of these things will make you rich alone, but they'll create a pattern. They'll place you in motion. They'll trigger a chain of events that compound quietly while others are still planning.

At first, it feels invisible. But the second you start showing up with something to give—even if it's tiny—the world tilts one degree in your direction. That's why the agent who makes ten calls a day eventually dominates. That's why the woman who launches her newsletter and keeps at it ends up with a brand. That's why the guy filming fly-fishing videos in a rented cabin ends up with a book deal. None of them aimed at wealth. They aimed at starting.

The lottery ticket is a seed too—but a weak one. It grows on fantasy, not effort. Some of those seeds sprout: a viral post, a crypto spike, a buyout. But the trees they grow rarely last. They're shallow. They can't handle weather. The better seed is boring. It's the $32 from your first online sale, the $8 affiliate commission, the $120 from helping someone fix their website. It looks small enough to laugh at, but don't. That's not a joke— that's a system forming. That's an invisible hand beginning to move.

Most people already hold a seed. They just dismiss it because it's small. But the power isn't in the size—it's in the planting. Once it's in the ground, your job isn't watching. It's doing. Water it. Feed it. Improve it. Expand the garden. Add more seeds. Don't count. Build. Wealth is never a single act. It's the repetition of one small act done consistently over time.

You don't need a financial planner as much as you need momentum. Enough motion to erase doubt. Start the podcast. Sell the first copy. Shake the first hand. List the property. Press record. Write the first page. It's not glamorous, but it's real— and real has a funny way of compounding when no one's watching.

Wealth hides in the work you almost didn't do: the post you almost deleted, the deal you almost didn't ask for, the idea you almost kept to yourself. Every large number you admire was once a small number someone refused to quit on.

Ignore the loud success stories—the "I run five companies" crowd sells flash, not foundation—and the lie their noise plants that small starts are beneath you or that you must think big from day one. That mindset kills momentum by confusing vision with pressure and convincing you to leap before you learn to walk, when real wealth never begins that way. It isn't complicated or mystical, but it is invisible until it isn't, and wealth begins with a small start that sneaks up on you if you let it.

Chapter 67 — Start the Side Thing

Nobody's coming to grant you permission. No one's going to slide a perfect opportunity across the table or tell you it's finally safe to start something for yourself. That's not how real momentum works. That's not how people break free. Most breakthroughs begin in secret—off-hours, in stolen time, on borrowed energy—while the rest of the world thinks you're doing something else.

This is for the person with a job, a family, and a life already full. You don't have to quit or burn everything down. You don't need a grand escape plan. You just need a sliver of energy and the courage to build something small that belongs to you. Start the side thing—the idea you keep pushing down, the website you bought and never touched, the YouTube channel you swore you'd launch, the product you outlined but never made, the book, the service, the skill. That thing.

It's not about fantasy. It's about leverage. In a world where you can't rely on stability, the side thing becomes your hedge against chaos. It's your test lab, your backup engine, your proof that you can create value outside a paycheck. Most people treat side projects like hobbies. I'm talking about something more serious—building a second engine while the first one's still flying.

Freedom isn't built with planning. It's built with proof. The side thing is proof that your value isn't locked inside a company or a job description. Starting it doesn't mean abandoning everything else. It means reclaiming forty-five minutes in the morning, the quiet hour before anyone wakes up, the edge of your lunch break. You build in the margins with low stakes and high truth. That's where real confidence grows.

There's a myth that "if it really mattered, I'd make time for it." That's false. You don't find time for important things—you steal it. You push something meaningless aside and dare the meaningful thing to grow. The side thing doesn't appear because you're ready; it appears because you start while you're not.

Most people think they need to go all in before they start. But that's another stall tactic. You earn the right to go all in by starting on the side. If your dream isn't worth doing quietly, it isn't worth doing loudly. And if you're waiting for validation before you act, you're giving away your agency.

The most successful builders I've known began in the cracks—investors running spreadsheets on lunch breaks, creators editing between shifts, founders testing prototypes after the kids were asleep. Real players don't wait for ideal conditions. They work with what they've got. The side thing sharpens your resourcefulness. It re-introduces you to hunger. When you stop leaning on a system for permission, you become the system.

And when something finally hits—even small—it's yours. That first sale or subscriber, earned in silence, is ignition. It's confidence that doesn't need applause. It just grows. Quietly. Steadily.

To find your side thing, start with the small irritations in your own life. A toothbrush that wears out too fast. A soap dish that never drains. Reading glasses that vanish every week. A better grill cleaner. A tool for sorting duplicate photos. An easier diet fix. These aren't billion-dollar ideas, but they're real

238

problems—and real problems attract real buyers. When one person pays to solve something you solved first for yourself, you'll never see the world the same way again.

I know a woman in Colombia, a single mother with a child to support and nothing fancy to work with. She started cooking lunches—one bowl, one dish, one price. Five dollars. That was it. Today she owns a warehouse, employs dozens, and feeds hundreds. No investors. No business plan. Just motion. That's what starting on the side can do.

The side thing doesn't have to look impressive. Some of mine didn't. One was a quiet service I never even listed online. I offered it one-on-one, tested it, kept it lean. It didn't scale, but it paid the bills while something else was dying. That "non-brand" kept me alive. That's the power of motion.

Side things aren't side forever. Some become main engines. Some stay small and perfect. Some morph into something better. But every one of them builds confidence. They shift identity—from employee to builder, from dependent to self-directed. They give you something to say yes to when the big thing collapses, because one day it might. And when it does, you'll already know how to build from scratch.

The side thing is also medicine for your mind. It gives you space to test ideas without high pressure. It lets curiosity breathe. It restores the part of you buried under survival mode. That's why it deserves respect—not as a joke, not as a "maybe someday," but as a small fire you protect in a windstorm.

It might be a blog, a product line, a book, a service, a newsletter, a local system, a software tool—it doesn't matter. Start it this week, this weekend, tonight, before the world

239

convinces you that now isn't the right time, because you don't owe anyone an announcement, just the action. The world doesn't need another perfect plan; it needs people willing to quietly build something that matters, to build leverage before they need it, courage before they're desperate, and something small that belongs entirely to them—and to start it on the side.

Chapter 68 — When You Don't Know How to Make Money, Start Giving

Let's be clear—this isn't about giving away your savings. It's not about writing checks, donating to charity, or throwing money at your problems. If you're broke or stuck financially, giving money is the last thing I'd recommend. This is about a deeper kind of giving.

When you don't know how to make money, you don't retreat. You don't shut down. You give something of yourself—your time, your creativity, your insight, your energy, your presence. Not because it's nice, but because it gets you moving again. Because giving is starting. And when life stalls, the only way to regain power is to move.

Scarcity makes you smaller. When you're worried about money, everything tightens—your thinking, your posture, your risk tolerance, even your faith. You start protecting instead of producing. You stop offering ideas, stop initiating, stop showing up. Scarcity doesn't just drain your bank account. It drains your spirit. It clouds judgment, shrinks your reach, and locks you inside your own fear. When that happens, you can't see opportunity because your energy points inward. That's why giving matters. Not because it's moral—but because it breaks the freeze.

You can give without spending a dime. You can give a recommendation, a connection, feedback, a ride, a compliment that actually lands. You can give ten minutes, one introduction, a little encouragement. You can lift the temperature of a room just by showing up with intention. You can serve before you sell. You can move before you monetize. If you want to shift your financial reality, stop waiting for income and start creating impact.

Giving flips the circuit. It turns energy from inward to outward, from "I need" to "I'm available." It sends a signal to the world—and to yourself—that you're still in the game. You're not hiding. You're leaning forward. Even when you don't know where it leads, you're willing to plant something. That alone changes your state. The world doesn't reward neediness. It rewards movement.

Most people think money is the only resource that matters. But early on, energy is the real currency. So is attention. So is presence. So is courage. When you walk into a room confident and curious, that's wealth. When you listen with focus, that's value. When you help someone else move forward, even before you have it all figured out, that's capital. You don't need cash to change your direction—you need circulation. And giving reopens the flow.

Everyone wants to monetize. They want the funnel, the link, the scalable offer. Fine. But momentum makes all of that easier. The fastest way to build momentum isn't to design a business model—it's to give something real. Give effort, give time, give clarity, give service. Once that starts moving, opportunities show up. People start asking how they can pay you. The path to income almost always begins with generosity.

I learned this the hard way. I've been stuck financially—sitting in frustration, scribbling offers, chasing "perfect" ideas. Nothing worked until I stopped thinking about what I could sell and started helping someone else win. One introduction.

One insight. One favor. And suddenly the static lifted. It didn't make me rich overnight, but it reconnected me to usefulness. And usefulness is the first step out of scarcity. When I gave, even a little, I stopped feeling poor. I felt in motion.

Money problems often come bundled with identity problems. You start thinking, I'm not valuable. I'm falling behind. I don't matter. Those are lies told by inertia. Giving breaks them. The moment you give, you prove you still have something to offer. You remember that you carry insight, presence, and perspective—even if you can't bill for them yet. Identity isn't what you claim; it's what you practice. When you practice generosity, you become someone who creates value long before revenue catches up.

And giving doesn't mean being used. It's not saying yes to everything or working for free forever. Giving is strategy. It's a targeted act of power—the power to move, to lift, to offer, to connect. You decide what to give, when, and to whom. You're not giving from desperation but from alignment. That's what starters do. They move even when their account balance says otherwise.

The effects show up faster than you think. People respond differently. You feel lighter. Ideas appear. A message comes through. Someone mentions your name. Confidence returns. The tone of your life shifts. Because now you're not asking what you can get—you're giving the world a reason to remember you.

Don't believe the myth that you need abundance to give. You already have something to offer: your focus, your insight, your willingness to help. What matters isn't how much—it's that it moves. The act of giving reactivates your agency.

Most people wait until they feel abundant to give, but maybe abundance begins with giving, with realizing that what you think you're missing may be waiting behind one act of contribution. Money rarely comes to those who chase it; it comes to those who move what they already have, so if you don't know what to do next and you're tired of waiting for clarity or rescue, give something—start moving, start helping, start showing up—because when you don't know how to make money, the worst thing you can do is freeze, and the best thing you can do is start giving.

Chapter 69 — Start with One Buyer

If you're in business and not making money, you're not in business—you're prepping. You're circling. You're avoiding. That's not an insult. It's a reckoning. People spend months, even years, building websites, tweaking logos, watching tutorials, and "working on" their offer. They act like entrepreneurs, but if you can't point to one real customer who's said yes, you haven't started yet.

You need one buyer. Not traffic, not followers, not subscribers. A buyer—someone who says, Yes, I trust you. Let's move forward. That first yes changes everything. It shifts you from potential to proof. The moment you earn that first commitment—a signed agreement, a check, a deposit— something inside you clicks. You're no longer thinking about business. You're doing it.

Most people don't start with one buyer. They start with a hundred excuses. I need my site finished. I need a better pitch. I'm not ready yet. These are delay tactics dressed as preparation. We hide behind polish because it feels safer than rejection. But clarity doesn't come from planning. It comes from contact.

You don't need branding to get a buyer. You don't need funnels, LLCs, or color schemes. You need one human being with a problem and the courage to offer a solution. The first buyer rarely comes from a campaign. They come from a conversation—a phone call, a text, a simple moment of truth where you say, Here's what I do. Want help? It feels too simple because it is. And simple works.

If you're in a results-based business like real estate, coaching, or consulting, the principle still applies. A buyer isn't always someone who pays today—it's anyone who commits to letting you help them. A signed listing agreement counts. A booked consultation counts. The first yes is still the start.

That yes is proof. Proof that what you offer lives in the real world and matters to someone besides you. That one buyer teaches you more about sales, service, and communication than any course you'll ever buy. They'll ask questions, raise objections, and test your process. That's your research lab.

When that buyer says yes, serve them completely. Deliver like they're your only client—because they are. If you do it right, that first deal becomes your origin story. It's the example you'll reference when the business grows and things get cloudy. That's your calibration point—the moment you stopped pretending and started producing.

Getting that first buyer also trains you to face rejection. The road to yes is paved with silence, ignored messages, and awkward calls. Most people quit there. They mistake friction for failure. But that friction is sharpening you. Every unanswered text builds your nerve. Every no gets you closer to yes. Eventually, someone responds. That's your door opening.

The surprise is how much energy that one yes gives you. It's not just confidence—it's identity. You stop needing validation because you have proof. You go from talking about business to doing business. One buyer becomes your foundation. And from that foundation, everything else—marketing, systems, scaling—finally makes sense.

I had a friend who spent years studying Microsoft software. He earned certifications in tools he never used, always "getting ready" for a consulting business that never existed. One day I asked, "What could you do for someone this week that would make their life easier?" He called a local business owner struggling with email chaos and offered to fix it—for free. Two hours later, he had his first fan. The owner said, "Can you come back next week?" That was it. Two hours. One yes. Within months, he had paying clients and a real business.

That's how it works. One buyer. One yes. That's the ignition. You don't need to be amazing—you need to be useful. Say what you offer. Back it up. Nothing fancy. Just real value in real time.

And if you're scared, good. Fear means you're close to something that matters. Most people live their whole lives one step away from their start. They almost launch. Almost pitch. Almost act. They "get ready" forever. But readiness is a mirage. You don't need fearlessness—you need movement.

If you're starting anything, stop hiding behind prep. Go have one real conversation. That's your start—not a campaign, not an announcement, just one human connection. One buyer. One yes.

From there, your only job is to repeat it—not scale, repeat— one yes per week, one problem solved at a time. The people who win aren't necessarily smarter; they just keep doing the simple things others abandon, showing up, asking, serving, closing, not talking about doing business but doing it. You don't need more theory or motivation; you need the next name, the next message, the next call, because that's how momentum

247

THE MAGIC OF STARTING

starts—one buyer at a time.

Chapter 70 — Start the Work Others Avoid

Most people are in the business of avoiding discomfort. They dress it up as strategy, trends, or tech stacks—but it's still avoidance. Especially in business. Especially in real estate. Talk to any modern consultant and you'll hear the same polished lines: Direct mail doesn't work anymore. Nobody answers calls. People don't want to be contacted. Build your brand first. It sounds smart. It feels modern. But it's a lie disguised as wisdom.

What they're really saying is: Don't do the hard stuff. Don't risk rejection. Don't make contact. Stay behind the screen and polish your image. Tweak your logo. Schedule another post. It's all a campaign to avoid the one thing that moves results—real effort in the real world.

And when you start to rise, you'll notice something strange: the mediocre voices all sound alike. They'll tell you what's dead, what's outdated, what doesn't work anymore. They say it with conviction, usually from the middle of the pack. That advice doesn't come from winners. It comes from the plateaued—from people who'd rather sound informed than be effective. Their language is code for "don't take risks." You can spot them easily—they're always managing, never moving.

You want to rise? Start with the work they avoid. Start with the phone call that might go nowhere. Start with the follow-up that feels thankless. Start with the blocked-out hour of grunt work. Start with the task that feels beneath you. Because that's where identity is forged. That's where respect is earned. Over time, that's where the edge is built.

I remember my first real estate interview—Coldwell Banker, thirty years ago. I was green and nervous. While waiting for the broker, I asked the secretary, "What does the average agent here make?" She looked at me, steady and unimpressed, and said, "Are you average?" I wanted to disappear. Never asked that question again. Average is a mindset—a quiet agreement with mediocrity. I had no intention of signing that one.

One of the top agents in that office was a woman. No flash. No noise. Just relentless motion. When I asked how she built her business, she'd shrug and say, "Darling, start with rentals," or "It's not your time yet." It sounded dismissive, but I stopped listening to her words and watched her work. She showed up every morning, walked her farm area, waved to neighbors, remembered names—even dogs. She didn't sell. She showed up. She did the work no one wanted to do—and owned that neighborhood because of it.

One Fourth of July, I saw her do something that burned into my mind. She placed a small American flag at every single home in her farm area. Hundreds of houses. Alone. No assistant, no applause, no shortcut. Just her, a bucket of flags, and summer heat. Most agents would've laughed at the idea—too much effort, no instant ROI. She didn't care. She understood what most never grasp: showing up in the real world matters more than showing off online.

She didn't outsource it or overthink it. She just did it. That's why she owned the market. She wasn't chasing leads; she was creating presence. Every homeowner saw her name not on a screen, but on their street. That's how a brand is built—in sweat, not pixels. That's what separates real pros from digital spectators. She didn't teach; she modeled. The lesson was simple: success lives in the work others avoid.

You don't need a strategy to begin. You need a will. You need to walk past the excuse factory and do the thing no one else wants to do. That's the real shortcut. That's the multiplier. Not a system or a hack—just the hard work that compounds quietly. And once you start, something changes. The task you dreaded becomes the task you dominate. Your edge sharpens. Your confidence stabilizes. You replace motivation with rhythm. You stop negotiating with yourself.

The hard tasks don't vanish, but they stop feeling hard as you stop asking what's trendy or scalable and start asking what actually moves the needle. No one claps when you pick up the phone, walk your block, or write the follow-up email, but in six months, a year, five years, those reps separate you—they make you calm under pressure, fast when others freeze, clear when others stall—until you become the one who doesn't flinch, all because you were willing to do what everyone else avoided.

Chapter 71 — A Parent's Guide to Starting

Kids aren't unfocused. They're un-started. Adults forget this because our brains have decades of scaffolding to get us moving: executive function, discipline, internal self-talk, habit structures. A six-year-old doesn't have any of that. Their attention moves like a school of minnows. One shift of light and the whole thing darts sideways. You can't lecture focus into a child. You can only model motion in front of them.

And I'll be honest—I didn't learn this because I'm naturally patient or gifted at parenting. I learned it because I tried the wrong approach first. I explained too much. I gave little speeches. I thought understanding would trigger action. It never did. Kids don't respond to lectures. They respond to demonstrations. They calibrate their energy to the first move they see you make. So you start for them.

I touched on this earlier when I wrote about starting with your kids, but it's worth repeating because it's the truth underneath everything: children don't move because you explain—they move because you begin. Your motion becomes their ignition.

When I took the training wheels off my kids' bikes, it wasn't a ceremony. There was no pep talk about courage or balance. It was quick and physical: hands on the seat, feet on the pedals, a gentle push. The first few feet were mine. The next twenty belonged to them. Once the wheels were turning, their bodies figured out what their minds never could have grasped through explanation. The hard part—the beginning—was handled. And once the beginning is handled, kids surprise you with how rapidly they take over.

That pattern showed up everywhere else—not because I designed some master parenting philosophy, but because I stumbled into something that worked. When my daughter was learning to write her name, I didn't give a mini lesson on letters. I wrote the first one and slid the pencil into her hand. When she wanted to draw, I'd sketch a simple line and she'd fill the page with her own ideas. When reading started to click, it was because I pointed to the first word and said it with her. Kids don't need pristine conditions or long explanations. They need ignition—the frictionless first inch that lets their brain latch onto the task.

Even something as simple as fishing worked this way. Instead of explaining how to cast, I'd cast once myself. A small, controlled motion. Their hands mirrored mine almost instantly. Motion beats instruction. Children learn through imitation long before they learn through explanation. Neuroscience backs this up: kids regulate their emotional and attentional states through social referencing—watching the adult to decide what to do next. Classic research from Campos and Stenberg showed that a child would cross a platform only when the parent's face signaled "go." The cue to begin came from the adult's state, not the child's confidence.

Learning theory says the same thing. Vygotsky called it the Zone of Proximal Development: kids learn best when an adult begins the task just slightly ahead of the child's current ability, then steps back. The child completes what was started. It's the foundation of almost every successful teaching moment. You initiate the motion, and the child, now inside the momentum you created, takes off.

I've seen it across everything—throwing a first pitch in the backyard, helping them start a simple prayer before bed, or having them give a tiny one-sentence "speech" at the dinner table. The structure is always the same: I begin, they continue. I remove the activation energy, they carry the flow. None of this came from expertise. It came from noticing what worked better than over-explaining or pushing.

Behavioral activation studies reinforce the entire pattern: action precedes motivation. Not the other way around. When you start the task with a child, you bypass the developmental lag in executive function they simply don't have yet. You lend them your momentum until their nervous system catches up. And over time, something powerful happens—they internalize the pattern. They begin to self-start because starting has never been a threat. It has always been a shared movement.

And here's the part I had to learn the hard way: you won't get it right every time. I didn't. I still don't. Some days I explain too much. Some days I lose patience. Some days I forget the simple truth that starting beats instructing. But when I remember—when I take the first inch instead of giving the first lecture—the entire dynamic shifts. Everything gets lighter. They move, and I don't have to push.

A child raised with easy beginnings becomes an adult who doesn't freeze at the edge of unfamiliar tasks, learning early that new things don't require confidence or readiness, only the first inch. Give a child enough first inches and they eventually begin offering their own, because kids don't need big lessons about motivation—they need motion, they need you to go first, clearly and calmly, showing the first move so they can grow into the rest. That's how you teach the magic of starting, not through speeches or perfection, but through one shared beginning at a time.

Chapter 72 — Start What You Want Others to Finish

Every group mirrors the energy of the first move. Every project inherits the tone of the first sentence. People rarely follow instructions; they follow motion. If you want something finished, don't delegate the vision—model the first stroke.

Most leaders confuse telling with starting. They outline goals. They assign tasks. They assume clarity will spark action. It won't. People don't move because you explained it well. They move because you showed them what movement looks like. They follow the momentum you create, not the words you say. You have to show them.

Lay the brick. Write the first paragraph. Make the first call. Solve the first bug. When others see your fingerprints on the work, they enter with a different posture. Not because they want to help you. Because you've made the finish line visible. You've shown them what "done" feels like.

This is how momentum scales.

Think of a seed. You don't yell at it to grow. You water it. You pull the weeds. You set the pattern. Most teams aren't slow— they're waiting for the pattern to begin. They're waiting for evidence that the work matters enough for someone to start it.

Look at the creators who give their editors the first ten seconds of a video so the tone is unmistakable. Or the coach who doesn't just design the drill but runs it—whistle around his neck, stopwatch in hand, sweat on his shirt. He takes the first shot, runs the first lap, shouts the first word of encouragement. He isn't managing from behind a clipboard. He's in the gym, setting the emotional temperature before the team even stretches.

The architect who sketches the first frame before passing it to design, the marketer who writes the subject line before handing off the campaign—these people aren't micromanaging. They're lighting the fuse. Don't say "run with it." Show what it means to run.

This approach isn't new. It's just forgotten. Decades ago, Hewlett and Packard led their company by walking the factory floor instead of hiding in conference rooms. They asked questions. They looked over shoulders. They caught small problems before they grew teeth. Their authority came from proximity—being close enough to see the real work, not the PowerPoint version of it.

Years later, researchers studying America's best-run companies kept finding the same pattern. The strongest cultures were led by people who stayed near the work. Not hovering. Not controlling. Just present enough to spark motion, remove friction, and make courage feel possible.

Today, that style of leadership looks outdated because dashboards replaced presence and remote culture made leadership abstract. But here's the truth: nothing kills energy faster than a leader who disappears behind a strategy doc. Presence multiplies effort. And nothing signals presence faster than starting something yourself.

You don't need to recreate old HP. You don't need clipboards or factory rounds. You just need to return to the core idea: start with your hands, not your mouth. You don't even have to be physically there. Upload a 15-second reference cut. Write the first three lines of a pitch in Slack. Open a client conversation with a handwritten question. Start the thing everyone else is afraid to start.

In the old model, managers reviewed what was done. In the new model, leaders set the first frame. Not to dictate style but to erase fear. A 2011 follow-up analysis to the original ego-depletion research found that people work longer and more consistently when the "activation energy" of starting is reduced. Not eliminated—reduced. A visible start lowers the cognitive cost for everyone else. Your first stroke removes resistance.

When you model the start, deadlines become shared instead of assigned. The final version stays closer to the original intent. You spend less time clarifying and more time shipping. And the team finally sees the real standard rather than the abstract one you talked about.

Even silence matters. Most people drown themselves in music while trying to work, believing it boosts productivity. But a 2019 study in *Applied Cognitive Psychology* found that whether music was familiar, unfamiliar, instrumental, or vocal, performance dropped compared to silence. Another experiment with 114 participants showed that both vocal and instrumental tracks reduced creativity. Silence consistently produced better originality and fluency.

Music feels productive because it hijacks your dopamine cycle. It gives you a quick reward without the effort that should earn it. You feel "good enough" to stop—even though you haven't moved anything forward. Real dopamine comes from forward motion. From the sentence you wrote. From the bug you solved. From the first call you made.

So make silence part of your starting ritual. Skip the soundtrack for the first twenty minutes. Don't reward yourself with noise until the page is no longer blank. Let the quiet carry weight.

And if the start feels too small, remember this: one sentence is enough. "I don't want to go to work today." "I'm avoiding the hard call." "That meeting drained me." That's not journaling— that's ignition. Once you type the line, your brain tilts forward. The same thing applies to emails, design files, CRM entries, strategy docs, product drafts. Add the title. Drop the placeholder image. Write the first bullet. Break the zero.

One sentence is proof—show people it's okay to begin, not with permission but with evidence, because this is more than leadership, it's leverage. The tiniest visible start carries more power than the loudest invisible plan, and that's why you're willing to be the person who types the first word.

Chapter 73 — Quiet Starts Change Cultures

There's power in a whisper. Some of the most defining shifts in momentum begin not with a roar but with a breath—barely audible, fully intentional. When everyone else is rushing, starting quietly becomes a form of leadership. When you repeat it, it becomes culture. Quiet is not the absence of action; it's the sharpening of intent.

You don't need to broadcast your next move. The most effective work—creative, personal, entrepreneurial—almost always begins with a single, precise action. A direct message. A handwritten note. One sentence typed into an empty document. The world rewards noise, but the builders—the people who actually move things forward—reward clarity. They use silence the way a craftsman uses a clean workbench: to see exactly what matters.

I learned this long before I understood why it worked. In my first semester of college, I coasted. Filled my schedule with fluff. Easy A's. Classes I didn't care about. I moved without direction. One afternoon before spring registration, I reached into my backpack and found a small, crumpled note in handwriting I didn't recognize. I still have no idea who wrote it or how it ended up there. It said: "No one's going to tell you what to take. You already know the classes that matter—so take them."

That line cut straight through me. I sat there holding that note like it was a flare in the dark. I dropped every easy class I had lined up and registered for the ones that scared me a little—the ones that made my pulse jump. There was no announcement, no reinvention, no external push. Just a quiet start that ended up reshaping the path I took for years.

Quiet starts work because they shrink the gap between intention and action. They don't invite overthinking. They don't require buildup. They don't trigger the internal alarms that accompany big, flashy commitments. They slide under resistance and give you one clear foothold. When you move from that foothold, you shift identity without theatrics.

Teams feel this too. A small design studio I know begins each morning with one question sent over Slack: "What's the one thing we can finish before noon?" Nothing tracked, nothing saved, nothing formal. But that single line sets the rhythm. A developer friend leaves one unfinished line of code open each night so the task pulls him forward the next morning. A founder I once coached kept an empty chair in every meeting to represent the customer. No speech. No introduction. Just a quiet anchor that re-centered the room every time.

Psychology backs this up. The Zeigarnik Effect shows that the brain clings to unfinished tasks far more than finished ones. An open loop creates tension, and the mind wants to resolve it. Baumeister's early research on cognitive tension points to the same truth: motion eases the strain faster than planning. This is why even starting—just typing a sentence, opening the email draft, laying out the tools—creates a gravitational pull toward completion. Quiet starts open loops without overwhelming the system.

People in different fields use this instinctively. An Etsy seller begins her day by rewriting the description of the item that's been ignored the longest. A copywriter whispers, "One clean line," and lets momentum take over. A realtor dials the hardest missed call from yesterday before hesitation builds. A gym owner resets the kettlebells before sunrise; that ritual grounds him and signals that the day has begun. A podcaster hits record and speaks the first honest sentence that comes to mind. A SaaS founder sends one thank-you message to a user before checking email. These aren't grand gestures. They're quiet calibrations that steer the entire day.

Quiet starts teach your nervous system one essential truth: I move things. Momentum isn't built through noise; it's built through motion. Once your body experiences the first move, resistance drops. You're no longer planning to begin—you've already begun. And when others see you start without posturing or hype, it challenges their inertia more effectively than any motivational speech. People copy simplicity. They copy clarity. They copy starters.

This is how culture shifts. Inside homes. Inside small teams. Inside companies. Culture doesn't change because of declarations or slogans. It changes because someone models a believable move—one that others can repeat. Quiet starts create a rhythm people can feel. They lower the bar to entry. They make forward motion contagious.

Quiet doesn't mean invisible; it means deliberate and precise, and that's how it spreads. Tonight, before you shut everything down, write one question on a notecard—"What can I start quietly tomorrow that will still matter a week from now?"—then start it with one move, no buildup, no fanfare, quiet enough that you can feel the intent and let the echo grow from there.

Chapter 74 — Start by Asking Twice

You've hit the wall: the unreturned email, the stalled project, the foggy tension that drains momentum. It bleeds into your schedule, your team, your confidence. You stare at the issue and freeze, waiting for the right tone or the perfect plan. But you don't need a framework or a script. You need one trigger that cuts straight through hesitation: ask the question—then ask it again.

The echo works because it forces presence. The first question lands; the second sharpens it. Directors do this instinctively— "Action... action!" Coaches clap twice to pull a drifting team back to center. The repetition isn't noise. It's ignition. It signals that hesitation is over and movement begins now, collapsing attention onto the task in front of you.

Repetition lowers resistance by collapsing indecision. Taking even a tiny action restores a sense of agency, and when that action is prompted twice, the effect compounds. The echo narrows the field of options until one choice becomes unavoidable. People don't stay passive when a question repeats; they step into the decision because the mind no longer has room to drift.

The power is in the double drop. Ask, then repeat: "What's our biggest blocker? What's our biggest blocker?" "Should we lower the price? Should we lower the price?" The second echo tightens the spotlight and presses the mind past ambiguity. It removes the illusion that more thinking will help and replaces it with the pressure to choose.

You see it everywhere once you start looking for it. A blogger stuck on a headline asks a friend, "Morning Routines That Work or Why Your AM Stalls—what grabs you? What grabs you?" and gets an answer in seconds. A podcaster whose guest cancels ten minutes before recording mutters, "Five-minute solo tip episode—go for it? Go for it?" and hits record instead of collapsing the schedule. One echoed question replaces an hour of spiraling because it forces movement before doubt can regain control.

One of my favorite examples came from a solo founder running a small sustainability newsletter. Subscriber growth had stalled. He brainstormed strategy docs, posted polls, drafted ideas—nothing moved him forward. One morning, frustrated, he wrote to his Slack group: "What single change drives one more subscriber today? What single change drives one more subscriber today?" Someone replied within minutes: move the signup CTA above the fold. He made the change immediately. Within two hours, three new subscribers came in. Weeks of planning did nothing. One echoed question changed the day.

Repetition only works if it's followed by immediate motion. In the sixty seconds after asking, assign ownership: "Jordan, update the landing page by two." Set a short regroup: "We'll check back in fifteen minutes." When the task is done, mark it. That acknowledgment locks the loop. Ask, assign, act—no delay.

Most frameworks fail because they invite hesitation disguised as structure. People nod, file the steps away, and return to the same stuck cycle. The echo doesn't wait. It forces clarity now. It pulls the decision into the present and removes the option to stall. This isn't communication; it's ignition.

You can adapt it to your rhythm. Creative teams clear fog by asking, "Spark the storyboard or scrap it—what's your call? What's your call?" Solopreneurs keep it blunt: "Finalize this sale or drop it—what's next? What's next?" Even alone, the echo works: "Send the email or rewrite the offer—what's the move? What's the move?" The words don't matter. What matters is repeating the question until action replaces hesitation.

The rules are simple: ask twice, choose one decision, act immediately, mark the result, and repeat the rhythm. Use it in meetings, morning huddles, or private moments when you feel stuck. The echo becomes a pivot point that cuts through fog and restarts motion. Identify one tension point in your life right now—an email you're avoiding, a price you haven't decided on, a stalled idea waiting for courage—and put the echo to work by asking twice and moving before hesitation has time to regroup.

Chapter 75 — Start With the One

It never happens in groups. Not really. The big shift—the real start—never comes from getting everyone aligned or waiting for perfect timing. It doesn't come from strategy sessions, team consensus, or the rituals people use to postpone the first move. It begins in silence. With one person. One action. One small, unimpressive motion that rewires everything downstream.

Starting is always a lonely thing, but lonely isn't weakness. Lonely is where real change lives. When you begin something honest, there's no ceremony, no applause, no spotlight. Just motion. And that motion—no matter how tiny—has leverage. Once you accept that, you stop waiting for backup. You stop asking for clarity. You stop needing anyone to believe in you, because you only need the one.

One call. One blog post. One client email. One ten-minute walk. One honest conversation. You don't need a system yet. You don't need a five-year plan. You don't need the perfect setup. You need something that moves—anything—and you need to do it now. Momentum comes from motion, not planning or visualizing. The start is where the weight shifts.

Most people don't start because they believe the myth of the many—the idea that conditions must align before the first step counts. That the calendar must be clear, the mood right, the confidence high. But the many only show up after the one has been claimed. The start happens privately. The scale happens later. You start with one, and the rest eventually follow.

We've been conditioned to think scale first. Metrics first. Audience first. It's backwards. Scale is a shadow cast by repetition, and repetition only exists because someone had the guts to make the first move without asking the room for permission. The one is the whole game because it ignites everything else.

I learned this years ago when I was overthinking a project into oblivion. I kept trying to "get it right," as if perfection was a precondition for beginning. A friend finally said, "You're thinking in packs. Start thinking in singles." I didn't get it at first. Then he broke it down: "Help one person. Sell one thing. Make one dollar. That's your way forward."

That line snapped everything back into focus. I didn't overhaul my process. I didn't fix the entire project. I took the smallest meaningful step in front of me. One email, one offer, one reach-out. And that tiny action created a ripple strong enough to break the stall. It wasn't glamorous or polished. But it was real.

That's the thing: the one is always real. You either picked up the phone or you didn't. You either opened the document or you let distraction win. You either walked into the room or stayed in the car. People complicate this because complication feels safe. They bury the beginning under templates, dashboards, planners, and color-coded goals. All smoke. Real change is unpolished, vulnerable, and small—the opposite of glamorous.

And let's be clear: if you're in business, money has to be part of your one. Not because money is the only goal, but because money is the signal. Every action should tilt toward revenue, even if it's tiny. Call a lead. Offer a product. Create a $10 download. Build a $29 mini-course. The smaller and more honest, the better. Don't separate "the start" from "the money." That's how people stay broke. Every micro-step should move you closer to a transaction. That's not greed—it's grounding.

Money isn't meaning. Money is proof. If you're building something and no money is moving, you're still in theory. When someone says, "I'm building a brand," the only real question is, "Where's the money?" Not to challenge their worth, but to challenge the idea itself. Money signals that something real, something chosen, now exists. Start with the smallest version of that signal.

I've watched countless people sit on brilliant ideas for years, thinking they were missing a plan when they were missing a single decision. And what finally moved them wasn't a big breakthrough. It was a sale. Even a tiny one. A $39 download. A $9.99 preorder. Something small enough to say, "This exists. I exist." The size didn't matter. The shift did.

Because the moment a result lands, the ground under you changes. You stop being a thinker. You become a builder. You stop narrating what you want to do. You start proving it. That emotional shift—from theory to action—is instant and irreversible once it happens.

But you can't let yourself slip back into abstraction. That's the trap. After a win, big or small, the temptation is to refine the system instead of working it. To reorganize instead of execute. To tune instead of move. Don't take the bait. Keep doing the one, every day. That discipline cuts through everything else.

One blog post. One follow-up. One offer. One referral ask.

One showing. One rep. Over and over until the stack of "one"s becomes a wall of undeniable progress.

This isn't a productivity trick. This is survival. This is how you win in a world drowning in distraction and perfectionism. You become dangerous the day you stop needing to feel good in order to move. You become unstoppable the day you stop waiting for the crowd and choose to walk alone.

That's the soul of starting: not confidence or optimism, but action without permission, and it's available to you right now. You don't need a clean desk, the right vibe, or a sign—you need one step that makes things more real than they were five minutes ago, because that's the mission, the discipline, and the birthplace of momentum. Start with the one, then do it again, and again, and again—not because it's easy, but because it works.

Chapter 76 — Don't Wait for the Title

Most people wait for permission. They wait to be chosen. They wait for the role, the rank, the clean name tag that signals they've finally "made it." They spend years hovering in place because they think they need external approval before they can make a real move. But the best starters don't wait for titles. They move before the world recognizes them. That's why they get ahead.

If you want to lead, start leading. If you want to create, start creating. If you want to teach, start teaching. The title comes later—maybe much later. Sometimes never. But the action is available right now.

This is where most careers stall. People tell themselves they're waiting for the right moment, the right job, the right circumstances. But they're actually waiting for someone else to grant them legitimacy. They want a gatekeeper to tap them on the shoulder and say, "Okay, now you're official." That moment almost never comes. Titles aren't handed to the starter; they're claimed by the mover.

Some of the most respected founders you've never heard of didn't wait for applause or investor validation. They bought the domain, filmed the rough intro video, wrote the first version, sent the cold emails, set the first meeting. They didn't act like CEOs—they acted. And in acting, they became. At first, they were nothing more than a name on a Gmail account or a phone number buried at the bottom of a homepage. No prestige. No press. But they moved.

The market doesn't crown you. It catches up to you. And when it finally does, it calls you by the role you already started playing.

The same truth applies in every craft. If you're waiting to be hired by a university or licensed by a board before you teach what you know, you'll wait forever. Great teachers start in hallways, kitchens, coffee shops, DM threads, and living rooms. They help one person. They answer one question. They post one idea. They teach without permission, and the world adjusts.

Your body doesn't know your job title. It only knows whether you're moving or not. You don't need to feel like a writer—you need to write. You don't need to feel like a creator—you need to publish. Every creator, coach, seller, and builder you admire began as an unknown with zero validation. They started anyway. Movement makes the case, not the certificate.

I learned this late but learned it hard. I was near the end of my MBA—three classes left, ninety percent done. Everyone around me was focused on the corporate climb: get promoted, land the better title, secure a seat controlled by someone else. That was the whole rhythm of the program.

Then we studied a report that changed everything. It showed that most millionaires and high-net-worth individuals weren't corporate executives at all. They weren't waiting in line for promotion cycles. They weren't collecting badges. They were solo entrepreneurs. Independent operators. People who didn't climb the ladder—they built their own.

The impact was immediate. It wasn't rebellion; it was clarity. I realized I didn't want to spend twenty years hoping someone would pick me. I didn't want to chase a title someone else controlled. And here's what made the moment sharper: I only had three classes left. Three. I could have coasted through another semester and collected the piece of paper. But the vision hit like a lightning bolt, and the consequences of waiting felt too strong to ignore.

I didn't want to waste another three months preparing for a life I didn't want. I felt the urgency to move now—not later, not next semester. Now. So I didn't sign up for the final classes. I walked away, fully aware of what I was giving up, and I decided to start my own business immediately. A real start, not a theoretical plan. No title, no ceremony, no guarantees. Just momentum.

That decision taught me the real rule: the start is the permission.

A young podcaster once asked me, "How do I become the next Joe Rogan?"
I told him, "Start talking. Then keep talking."
He didn't like that answer. He wanted tactics, hacks, a ladder to climb. But there is no ladder. A voice isn't handed to you—you build it through output. You show up, you speak, you write, you make things, you help people. One day you look up and realize you became the thing you were chasing.
Don't wait for the title. Start. Let the title catch up.

When you walk like an author, write like an author, and publish like an author, you become one. When you act like a business owner, you are one. Recognition is delayed. Action isn't. Start before you're ready. Start before they notice. Start before they clap. That's how it becomes real. That's how it becomes yours.

There's one more move most people miss: name yourself. Not publicly. Not in your bio. Name yourself privately in a way that hits you in the chest. Don't pick corporate labels—they're costumes. Pick something meaningful, original, something that shifts your posture.

Call yourself The Builder, The Finisher, The One Who Ships, The Quiet Hammer, The First Mover, The Closer—pick the identity that straightens your back, whisper it, carry it, and use it when resistance hits. Then earn it through action, not announcements, bios, or validation games, because you don't need a title to begin—you just need to begin like someone who already owns it.

PART VII — Sustaining the Start

Chapter 77 — The Start Is Always Available

Most people live as if the window for starting has already slammed shut. They convince themselves they're too late, too old, too far behind. They talk themselves into believing the chance is gone. But here's the truth: the start is always available. Always. The gift of beginning again doesn't expire. Grace doesn't vanish just because you coasted too long.

I know this because I coasted for years. I wasn't failing. I was doing fine—and that's the danger. Good is the enemy of great. Failure hurts enough to wake you up. Good lulls you into a quiet coma. When you're failing, you know you need a new start. When you're "good," you can drift for decades, mistaking comfort for progress. You don't crash—you coast. And coasting is sometimes worse than failure because it blinds you to the fact that you've stopped climbing.

That's why I know the start is always available. Because looking back, I could have raised my standards sooner. I could have demanded more of myself earlier. But the gift doesn't disappear because you were late. Grace doesn't evaporate just because you drifted. The start waits—calmly, quietly—until you reach for it.

Behavioral science backs this up. Katy Milkman and her team at Wharton studied what they call the "fresh start effect." People were more likely to launch goals after temporal landmarks: birthdays, new years, Mondays. Those dates created a psychological separation—old me versus new me. It gave people permission to begin again. They waited for the calendar to tell them it was acceptable.

But here's the uncomfortable truth: the calendar doesn't own your fresh start. You don't need Monday. You don't need January 1st. You don't need a milestone birthday. The start is available at all times because the gift of beginning again is constant. The study simply revealed what we already know deep down—we're waiting for excuses when grace has been there the whole time. The restart button isn't tied to dates. It's tied to decision.

And if you want a living example of what that looks like in motion, watch Dave Wottle in the 1972 Munich Olympics. He lined up for the men's 800 meters wearing a golf cap pulled low, looking more like a weekend jogger than an elite runner. The gun fired, and within seconds he dropped to dead last. At 200 meters, still last. At 400, still last. The announcers practically wrote his obituary mid-race.

But Wottle wasn't done. With 300 meters to go, he started quietly reeling in the field—smooth, calm, almost casual. He picked off one runner, then another. With 100 meters left, he was suddenly in striking distance. And in the last 20 meters, he surged past the leaders, chest forward at the tape, winning Olympic gold.

That wasn't luck. That was belief in the start. Wottle didn't let a terrible beginning define his finish. He didn't decide the race was over just because he was behind. He understood that the start remains available even in the middle of the race. Grace doesn't care how late you were off the line. It only cares whether you're willing to move now.

And it's not just athletes who prove the point. Frank Lloyd Wright is another example. By the time most people are shrinking into smaller lives, Wright was still drawing bold lines on paper. He created some of his greatest buildings when most men his age were settling into retirement. Fallingwater—one of the most iconic homes in history—came in his late sixties. The Guggenheim Museum was completed when he was well into his eighties. People half his age had long since given up their creative edge, but Wright kept beginning. The start stayed available, and he kept taking it.

Then there's Colonel Harland Sanders. His story wasn't clean—it was messy. Farmhand. Streetcar conductor. Soldier. Gas station operator. Failed ventures. Decades of middling outcomes. Most people at that age decide it's too late. They lock themselves into decline. But Sanders didn't. In 1952, at sixty-two years old, with little more than a fried chicken recipe and stubborn belief, he began franchising what would become Kentucky Fried Chicken. He knocked on doors, slept in his car, pitched strangers, and endured rejection after rejection. At an age when most people seek comfort, he sought a beginning—and he found one. By the time he died, his face was on buckets worldwide.

These stories hit because they expose a truth we try to ignore: it's not too late. The start doesn't disappear with age or missed chapters.

Maybe that's why I've always had a soft spot for these stories. Because I know what it means to be late. Late to graduate. Late to marry. Late to have children. Every one of those could have been framed as "too late." But grace doesn't run on the world's clock. The start showed up when I was ready, and every new beginning came when I finally chose it.

That's why I can tell you this with certainty: the start doesn't punish you for delay. It doesn't mock you for drifting. It doesn't disappear because you coasted too long. The start is infinite. As long as you're breathing, the door remains unlocked.

The real danger isn't missing the start. The danger is believing the lie that you can't start again. Shame welds the door shut if you let it. Shame says you wasted too much time, so you don't deserve another beginning. But shame doesn't control the start. Grace does. And grace doesn't care about your wasted years. Grace cares about whether you'll move now.

So if you ever feel like you've missed your chance, remember this: the start is always available, and the gift of beginning again is still waiting for you—call it grace, renewal, or a second wind, whatever name you choose. The truth remains the same: it's never too late to begin again.

Chapter 78 — Start Even When It Doesn't Count

Most people only start when the lights are on. When the game is official. When the crowd is watching. When it finally "counts." But greatness isn't built in those moments. It's built long before the scoreboard, in starts that don't matter to anyone else—starts that are invisible, unrecorded, and easy to dismiss.

Think about the alleys of Buenos Aires where Diego Maradona learned to play. Long before stadiums, trophies, or global fame, he was a boy juggling a ball on dirt patches, weaving past friends in cramped streets, kicking a rag ball when money was tight. None of those games carried weight. No scout cared. But every touch was a start, and every start stacked. By the time the world noticed him, he had already begun thousands of times in places that looked like nothing.

Or take Colombia, long before it was known for elite climbers. Boys pedaled to school in the Andes because that was life. Egan Bernal grew up in Zipaquirá riding a second-hand bike up mountain roads most people wouldn't attempt for sport. No stopwatch. No coach. No medals. Just daily climbs that burned lungs and legs into something durable. Those miles didn't register publicly, but they built a body and a mind capable of winning when the stakes finally appeared.

Sports make the lesson obvious because the outcomes are visible, but the same structure shows up everywhere else.

Albert Einstein wasn't reshaping physics from a prestigious lab.

He was a patent clerk in Bern, reviewing other people's inventions and scribbling equations during breaks. To the academic world, those notes meant little. They weren't published. They weren't praised. But they seeded the theory of relativity. The start didn't matter to them. It mattered to him.

The pattern repeats in creative work. J.K. Rowling wasn't building a literary empire when she was writing in cafés with her baby beside her, exhausted and broke. Those pages didn't convince publishers or pay rent. They didn't signal success. But they were starts—and those starts built a universe that later reached millions.

Behind every visible win sits a long stretch of invisible preparation. Painters sketch studies no one will ever frame. Musicians grind scales in empty rooms. Writers fill notebooks with sentences that will never be read. None of that counts publicly, but it counts privately. That's where craft is built, long before confidence or permission arrives.

Business follows the same logic. Soichiro Honda didn't begin with a global company. He started in a tiny workshop making piston rings that mostly failed inspection. Toyota rejected him. Those early attempts didn't impress the market, but they shaped the judgment and resilience that later defined Honda Motor. The failures weren't wasted starts—they were formative ones.

Psychologist Anders Ericsson described this as deliberate practice: mastery doesn't arrive in one revealing moment. It emerges from thousands of small starts repeated when no one is watching. Those starts build the foundation. When the moment finally arrives, you're not beginning—you're

THE MAGIC OF STARTING

Most people fail because they wait for it to matter before they move. They wait for higher stakes, official conditions, or external validation. But if you haven't practiced starting when nothing seems to be on the line, you'll freeze when something finally is. The people who rise under pressure are the ones who already began quietly, repeatedly, and without witnesses.

Every hidden start stacks. Every invisible effort compounds. The world celebrates the visible moments, but lives are shaped in unseen places—the alleys, mountain roads, back rooms, notebooks, and kitchens where people build an edge long before anyone is watching. That's where capability is formed, confidence is earned, and greatness actually begins.

Chapter 79 — What God Starts, He Finishes

Some beginnings feel bigger than us. You can't explain them, you can't trace them, and you can't shake the sense that something placed the start in your hands. Call it design, call it providence, call it wiring—whatever word you choose, the pattern is the same: when something real begins, it carries a pull toward its own completion. The start comes with direction built into it, like a frequency only you can hear.

People think finishing is about willpower or talent or some heroic burst of discipline at the end. It's not. Finishing starts in the beginning. The beginning is the signal—the spark, the internal shift that says, "This matters enough to move." When a start is real, it whispers the next step. Not the whole plan—not yet—but the very next step, often with surprising clarity.

Some moments don't feel optional. They feel assigned. The business you can't stop thinking about. The conversation you know you need to have. The book you've carried for years. The version of yourself you feel rising even when your circumstances don't match it yet. These starts don't arrive every day, but when they do, you feel their weight. You don't choose them casually. They choose you.

Psychologists call these "self-concordant goals," the kind that feel internally given rather than externally imposed. In studies by Kennon Sheldon at the University of Missouri, people were far more likely to persist—and finish—goals that felt aligned with their identity. Not goals meant to impress others. Not goals designed to check boxes. Goals connected to who they were becoming. The stronger the alignment, the stronger the follow-through.

This is why some starts feel spiritual even if you're not religious. There's a sense of being guided, a sense that the idea didn't come from nowhere, that it was placed there. And once you step into it, the momentum feels different. You're not forcing something artificial—you're stepping into something that fits.

You've felt this before. The instant you finally commit, everything shifts. Hesitation loosens its grip. The resistance you've carried for months softens. It's not that the work gets easy—it's that the direction becomes clear. You still have to climb, but the mountain stops feeling random. It feels intended.

Some people confuse this with confidence. It isn't confidence. It's alignment. It's the feeling that you're saying yes to work that was always yours. It's the sense that you're not inventing the path from scratch—you're uncovering it step by step, like brushing dirt off a trail that was already there.

I've seen this across every area of life. Someone drifts for years, then one day something lands so heavily they can't ignore it. They start the business. They finally apologize. They get healthy. They leave the relationship they've been afraid to walk away from. They write the chapter. They lift the weight. They pick up the phone. From that moment forward, everything moves differently. It isn't magic. It's momentum born from a start that was overdue.

People get stuck because they want the whole arc before they take the first step. They want God, or life, or fate to show them the ending. But that's not how beginnings work. The world doesn't hand you the blueprint—it hands you the doorway. Your job isn't to predict the ending. Your job is to honor the beginning.

There's a quiet power in trusting this. You stop performing. You stop bargaining with yourself. You stop asking for guarantees. Instead, you step forward because the start was placed in your hands, and you feel responsible for it. That responsibility isn't heavy—it's grounding. It pulls you out of confusion and into motion. And motion reveals what planning never will.

People also misunderstand the relationship between grace and progress. They think grace is soft, passive, forgiving without expectation. But real grace is directional. Real grace offers a beginning and expects movement. Real grace says, "Here's another shot—now do something with it." The start is the invitation. The finish is the expression of gratitude.

Grace is patient. It doesn't vanish because you drifted too long. It doesn't scold you for being late. It doesn't shame you for wasted time. It waits. Your start waits. It sits quietly until you're ready to reclaim it.

What God starts, He finishes. And what's meant for you will keep whispering back until you move.

The real danger isn't abandoning the finish. The real danger is refusing the start. People stall their lives waiting for permission, waiting for signs, waiting for certainty. But the sign is the start itself. The fact that it keeps returning to your mind is the sign.

You don't need to be perfect to honor a beginning. You don't need confidence. You don't need a clean desk, a perfect plan, or a peaceful season of life. Every meaningful start I've ever taken came in a messy moment, with imperfect tools and doubts still clinging. But the act of starting wiped those doubts away. Clarity comes from movement, not from stillness.

The start you're avoiding—the one you keep pushing aside— that's the one that matters. That's the one carrying the finish. If it didn't matter, it wouldn't keep returning. If it weren't yours, it wouldn't keep tugging at you.

Your life changes when you stop asking whether you're ready and start asking whether the beginning is real. If it's real, honor it. Move. Start the thing placed on your heart. Start the thing that scares you because it matters. Start the thing that keeps resurfacing in quiet moments. Start the thing that feels like assignment, not suggestion.

Because what's meant to begin through you is meant to be finished through you. And the moment you begin, the rest starts lining up behind you.

Chapter 80 — Start Again and Again

Most people overvalue the first start. They treat it like a cinematic turning point—the dramatic moment when everything finally changes. But the truth is far more human: the people who win aren't the ones who start once. They're the ones who learn how to start again. And again. And again. No theatrics, no guilt, no self-destruction every time the rhythm breaks.

Real durability comes from your relationship with restarting. If you depend on perfect momentum, you won't last. If you depend on motivation, you won't last. If you depend on unbroken streaks, you won't last. Momentum always breaks. Streaks always break. Life always interrupts. Everyone drifts, everyone stalls, everyone loses focus. The difference between those who build something meaningful and those who don't is simple: the builders know how to recover quickly.

Most people attach shame to falling off. Miss a day? They panic. Miss a week? They collapse. Miss a month? They rewrite the story of who they are. Shame doesn't just slow progress—it kills restarts. And without restarts, nothing survives.

Here's the truth: restarts aren't failures. They're the system. They're the mechanism by which anything important survives the chaos of real life. The people you see as disciplined aren't living flawless streaks—they've learned how to re-enter the work without turning a slip into a catastrophe.

The fantasy of linear momentum destroys more goals than setbacks ever will. Momentum isn't linear. It comes in waves.

There will be long stretches where the work feels flat, dull, repetitive. People assume boredom means they're on the wrong path. It doesn't. Boredom is part of the path. Passion fades, excitement evaporates, and the ones who survive the plateau are the ones who restart inside boredom.

This is where the science becomes useful. Research on "habit discontinuity" by Bas Verplanken shows that people reset habits more effectively after disruption than during stability. Vacations, stress, seasonal shifts—those breaks don't ruin habits; they create openings for stronger ones. The restart window is often the most powerful moment you get.

This flips the emotional script. Instead of seeing a break as proof of failure, you see it as a chance to rebuild with more clarity, more intention, more self-respect. Once restarting becomes normal, shame loses authority. You stop catastrophizing. You stop spiraling. You stop acting like a slip defines who you are. You simply begin again.

Restarting builds identity faster than perfect consistency ever will. When you restart after boredom, you learn boredom can't stop you. When you restart after doubt, you learn doubt can't stop you. When you restart after a rough week, you learn the week didn't define you. Every restart rewires a belief: I move even when conditions aren't ideal.

That's real strength. That's real confidence. That's real identity change.

This is the chapter worth marking up. Highlight it. Write in the margins. Circle the lines that hit you. The skill you build here will carry every chapter of your life—financial goals, fitness, creative work, relationships, personal rebuilds. Because the truth is simple: you don't stay consistent by being flawless. You stay consistent by making restarts easy.

Forget perfect streaks. Perfect streaks create fragile confidence—one slip and the whole self-image collapses. Durable people don't worship streaks. They worship return. They know true consistency isn't the absence of breaks; it's the refusal to quit because of them.

If you restart ten times in a year, you'll outperform the person who makes one big January start and burns out by March. If you restart every month, you'll outpace the person waiting for motivation to return. If you restart every week, you become dangerous.

Restart immediately. Restart imperfectly. Restart without ceremony. Restart without apologizing to yourself. You're not rebuilding the runway—you're stepping back onto it.

This is how reputations are rebuilt, how bodies are rebuilt, how businesses are rebuilt, how confidence is rebuilt. Over years, repeated starts become the quiet backbone of an entire life. They teach you that you don't need ideal conditions to move. You don't need inspiration. You don't need certainty. You need honesty, followed by motion.

Here's the scientific anchor that matters most: research from Angela Duckworth and her team shows that grit isn't constant effort—it's consistent re-effort. The willingness to reapply yourself after setbacks predicts long-term outcomes more accurately than talent, resources, or even discipline. Not sustained force. Repeated force.

That's the engine of your future. Your life will be built on dozens of returns, not a single dramatic beginning—that's the truth behind every comeback story, every reinvention, every late bloomer. It was never one heroic act but thousands of quiet re-entries, starting again and again and again, not because you failed, but because this is how you win.

Chapter 81 — The Start Tool

Starting isn't just a mindset—it can be engineered. Every craft has its instruments. A carpenter has a hammer. A surgeon has a scalpel. A pilot has a checklist. When it comes to beating hesitation, drift, and indecision, you need your own instrument: a Start Tool. The mistake people make is waiting for motivation. That's like a carpenter walking onto a jobsite hoping a hammer will magically be lying around. Tools don't appear on their own. You bring them. You maintain them. You use them whether you feel like it or not.

A Start Tool isn't mystical. It's practical. It's what you reach for the moment resistance shows up. Some tools are verbal, like a Start Signal you've practiced. Some are physical, like sneakers by your bed. Some are environmental, like a cleared desk with only one task left on it. The purpose is the same in every case: you don't leave starting up to chance. You preload the action.

Tools work because they shrink the gap between intention and motion. The smaller that gap, the less oxygen hesitation has to grow. Think about the five-second window of resistance. If you don't act immediately, hesitation expands. A Start Tool closes that window. The countdown hack is a simple example: 3-2-1—move. There's no negotiation after "one." Tools eliminate willpower from the equation. You don't debate. You deploy.

The psychology is clear. BJ Fogg's model at Stanford shows that behavior occurs when motivation, ability, and a prompt converge. Motivation rises and falls. Ability stays relatively stable. Prompts—the triggers that launch action—are fully designable. That's what a Start Tool is: a deliberately engineered prompt. Fogg's research shows that even with low motivation, the right prompt still produces action. That's why habit stacking works. Brush teeth → floss. Alarm rings → run. Sit in chair → write. A Start Tool is a custom prompt built for your specific friction point.

There are clear categories. Physical anchors include shoes at the door, a filled water bottle, dumbbells beside your desk. Their presence kills the "later" excuse. Verbal triggers include Start Signals—personal lines that bypass doubt and collapse resistance into a single move: "Just the start." "Dial one." "Open the document." Environmental structures include phones in another room, desks cleared the night before, browser blocks during writing hours. The tool is the structure you design, not just an object.

The best Start Tools are boring. A hammer isn't exciting, but it hits the nail every time. A Start Tool should work on the hundredth day as well as the first. Hemingway engineered his own by stopping mid-sentence so the next morning the start was already built in. He never faced a blank page. That was his tool. Tools can dull over time. A countdown might lose its punch. A Start Signal might fade. That isn't failure—it's maintenance. Sharpen your tools. Rotate them. Evolve them. As the battle changes, the tools must adapt.

To build your Start Tool, pick one domain—not your entire life. Where's the friction? Getting out the door? Picking up the phone? Opening the document? Collapse only that choke point. If running is the goal, sleep in your workout clothes. If sales is the goal, put a Post-it on your desk that says "Dial One." If writing is the goal, leave the document open the night before.

A friend of mine wanted to return to drawing. Inspiration never came. Pressure froze him. So he built a tool: a sketchpad by his pillow. Each morning, he drew one line before his feet touched the floor. One line became two. Two became full pages. The tool did the real work. It created the start. Inspiration followed action, not the other way around.

Peter Gollwitzer's research on implementation intentions proves this scientifically: "If X happens, I will do Y." His studies showed that specifying the when-where-how nearly doubled follow-through. That's exactly what a Start Tool does. Shoes by the bed mean, "If the alarm rings, I run." A Start Signal means, "If resistance appears, I speak this line and move." The brain loves if-then shortcuts.

You see Start Tools in high-performance environments everywhere. Navy SEALs use rituals before breaching doors. It isn't superstition—it's engineered activation. Michael Phelps had a race routine so precise that by the time he reached the pool, the start was already complete. These aren't motivational tricks. They're structured starts.

Tools are shortcuts. They bypass the long road of doubt and take the direct path to motion. Rituals exist in every culture for the same reason. Monks with bells. Athletes with warm-ups. Pilots with checklists. All Start Tools. In health: shoes by the bed, playlist queued, water bottle filled. In business: one number on a Post-it, a cleared desk, an inbox timer. In creative work: a notebook left open mid-sentence, a guitar already tuned. In relationships: a reminder to send a message, phones in a drawer at dinner. These are small. That's why they work.

If you take nothing else from this book, take this: build your

Start Tool tonight. Not tomorrow. Not after motivation returns. Pick the one action you've been avoiding and forge the tool that cracks it open. A Start Tool isn't glamorous. Nobody brags about a hammer. But without it, nothing gets built. Your projects, your health, your business—all of it depends on motion.

You don't need motivation to fall from the sky. You need a tool in your hand. When you understand that, you stop waiting for magic and start carrying your own.

Chapter 82 — Start Forever

Some people never had to start. They were handed the position, born in the right room, given the microphone before they earned the silence. That doesn't make them bad. But it makes them different. Because if you've never faced the unknown, never lifted the first brick, never initiated momentum in a world that wasn't moving, you don't really understand what a start is.

But you do.

You've started something before—a job, a family, a move across the country, a letter you were scared to write, a prayer whispered because you didn't know what else to do. You started at a moment when everything in you wanted to wait. And you didn't start because you had advice or because you were ready. You started because something whispered: *go anyway*.

That whisper may have come from God, or your child, or your future self. But you heard it—and you moved. And that's why you're dangerous now. Because you know what it feels like to begin without guarantees.

Starting is sacred. It's more than motion, more than motivation. It's how you declare you're still alive, still listening, still becoming. It isn't a warm-up phase or something you graduate from. The moment you stop starting, you begin to decay—not in body, but in will, in spirit, in momentum.

This book was never about productivity. It was about

remembering who you are.

You've always had the power to start. This book simply gave it structure—a name, a shape, something to grab when the fog rolled in. But don't confuse the system for the source. Your Start Signal isn't mine. It's yours. It lived in you long before these pages existed.

If you've ever felt that voice calling you forward, you already know the truth: you don't need to feel powerful to start. You just need to move. The power comes after.

Most people believe the world is full of finishers. It isn't. The world is full of floaters—people carried into position by money, systems, parents, algorithms, or timing. They finish what was already in motion, but they don't start. Starting is different. Starting means creating something where nothing existed before. It's choosing friction over comfort. It's pulling the first car of a train when the rest of it is dead weight.

My grandfather, Abuelo Pepe, taught me this without ever trying to be profound. He once told me a locomotive pulls a train one car at a time. The engine doesn't yank the whole line; it tugs the first coupling, then the next, then the next. Momentum is distributed by sequence. That's how real things move.

He taught me more than metaphor. As a kid, he drilled me on the capitals of every U.S. state, then every country in the world. One by one. No shortcuts. No skipping the hard ones. He wanted me to understand something simple: you don't master a list—you start with the first entry, then the next. Competence is earned through sequence, repetition, and restarting every time

THE MAGIC OF STARTING

you forget.

And so it is with you.

You may not have a title. You may not have a platform. You may not have followers, funding, or validation. But you have the most powerful force on earth: the ability to start anyway. The humility to begin. The vision to act without applause. The courage to look foolish for a moment so you don't stay stuck for a lifetime.

That's what makes you rare.

You don't need a roomful of people to tell you what comes next. You don't need credentials to take the next step. You don't need applause to begin the work that matters. You already know what the next start is.

And if you forget, start again.
If you fail, start again.
If you're misunderstood, dismissed, or underestimated—start again.

Start in quiet. Start in small rooms. Start with what's in your hand. Start when it's inconvenient. Start when nobody is watching. You don't need someone else's system, timing, or belief. You have your own. And when that faith feels small— mustard-seed small—all you have to do is place it in the soil. That's the start. And that's enough.

You never outgrow the start. You return to it. You rebuild with it. You carry it like fire. The more you honor the start, the less you'll be seduced by the finish. Don't mistake visibility for virtue. Don't confuse loudness with leadership. Don't let your gift rot on the vine while you wait for permission.

You already have permission.

No gatekeeper stands between you and your next start. Only inertia. Only noise. Only the lie that you need more advice. But you don't. You need one thing: one small act, one short phrase, one Start Signal. And motion begins again.

So let others polish what they were handed. Let them chase prizes you never asked for. You start. Then you start again. Because the ones who start without needing approval aren't just creators or leaders.

They're free.

Before You Go

If you've made it this far, the book didn't rush you.
It asked you to stay with one idea long enough to let it settle.

Most books ask you to remember things. This one asked you to notice something you already live with every day: the quiet moment before action, where almost everything meaningful either begins—or doesn't.

You don't need to do anything dramatic after this. There's no identity to adopt, no overhaul required, no pressure to perform. The system in this book doesn't need to be installed. It only needs to be used.

There is likely one small thing you've been circling. Something useful. Something generous. Something that would clearly add value—to your work, your skills, your income, or the people around you—but keeps getting delayed because it doesn't feel ready yet.

That's the moment this book is for.

Starting isn't about committing to a new identity. It's about choosing a next action that is small, specific, and well-designed enough to bypass motivation entirely. Once motion begins, momentum follows. Not because you forced it—but because that's how progress works.

You don't need to protect the start. You don't need to dramatize it. You don't need permission.

The next start will happen either way. This book simply gives you a way to choose it instead of defaulting past it.

If the book worked, you won't feel pressure right now. You'll feel clarity—and a slight pull toward one thing that's been waiting quietly in the background.

That's enough.

Close the book when you're ready. Let it sit. Come back to it when something stalls. Use it as a reference, not a rulebook.

What matters isn't finishing chapters or remembering lines. What matters is whether something that didn't begin before… begins now.

Everything big still begins small.

One Small Ask

If this book was useful to you, there's one small thing you could do that helps more than you might expect.

Leave a brief review.
Most readers leave one right after finishing, while it's still fresh.

It doesn't need to be long. A sentence or two is enough. You don't need to explain everything or say it perfectly. Just an honest note about whether the book helped you think differently or take a step you might not have taken otherwise.

You can leave your review here:

themagicofstarting.com/review

If you do leave a review, I'll count that as a start.
Not a big one. Just a small, intentional action that makes something easier for the next reader who's standing where you once were.

Thank you for reading.
And thank you for beginning.

About the Author

James Salas writes about momentum, discipline, and the mechanics of starting when conditions are imperfect and clarity is incomplete. His work focuses on small, repeatable actions—the kind that quietly shape outcomes over time without relying on motivation, drama, or certainty.

Over the years, he observed that the moments that changed direction were rarely breakthroughs. They were starts: modest actions taken before confidence arrived, repeated long enough to compound. That observation became the foundation for this book.

The same principles apply across scale. They work for personal projects, habits, and career decisions, and they work just as reliably in large, complex efforts like development, construction, and software—anywhere progress depends less on inspiration and more on starting correctly.

Salas continues to write and build systems that explain how progress actually happens, especially when waiting feels easier than beginning.

Other Books by the Author

The Call of the Creek

www.ingramcontent.com/pod-product-compliance
Lightning Source LLC
Chambersburg PA
CBHW062044080426
42734CB00012B/2552